CONFLICT, BALANCE, BREAKTHROUGH

CONFLICT, BALANCE, BREAKTHROUGH

THE CHOICE IS YOURS

DAVID WILLARD
WITH GRETCHEN WILLARD

Published by David Willard: www.conflictbalancebreakthrough.com

Scriptures that are not referenced are from the King James Version of the Bible. Public
Domain.

Scripture quotations marked (NASB) are taken from the New American Standard Bible®,
Copyright © 1960, 1962, 1963, 1968, 1971, 1972, 1973, 1975, 1977, 1995 by The
Lockman Foundation. Used by permission. (www.Lockman.org)

Scripture quotations marked (NIV) are taken from the HOLY BIBLE, NEW
INTERNATIONAL VERSION®. NIV®. Copyright© 1973, 1978, 1984 by International
Bible Society. Used by permission of Zondervan. All rights reserved.

Scripture quotations marked (TNIV) are taken from the HOLY BIBLE, TODAY'S NEW
INTERNATIONAL VERSION®. TNIV®. Copyright© 2001, 2005 by International Bible
Society. Used by permission of Zondervan. All rights reserved.

Scripture quotations marked (NASB) are taken from the NEW AMERICAN STANDARD
BIBLE®, Copyright © 1960,1962,1963,1968,1971,1972,1973,1975,1977,1995 by The
Lockman Foundation. Used by permission.

Scripture quoted by permission. Quotations designated
(NKJV) are from THE HOLY BIBLE: NEW KING JAMES VERSION.
Copyright © 1982 by Thomas Nelson Inc.
All rights reserved.

Scripture quotations marked (NLT) are taken from the Holy Bible, New Living Translation,
copyright 1996, 2004. Used by permission of Tyndale House Publishers, Inc., Wheaton,
Illinois 60189. All rights reserved

Noah Webster 1828 Dictionary. Permission to reprint the 1828 edition granted by G&C
Merriam Company. Copyright 1967 & 1995 (Renewal) by Rosalie J. Slater. Published by the
Foundation for American Christian Education.

Willard, David, 1971-
Conflict, balance, breakthrough: the choice is yours
/ by David Willard.
p. cm.
Includes bibliographical references.
ISBN-13: 978-0-615-26447-9
ISBN-10: 0-615-26447-6

1. Conflict management--Religious aspects--
Christianity. 2. Christian life. 3. Christian life--
Biblical teaching. I. Title.

BV4597.53.C58W55 2009   248.4
                            QBI09-600006

ISBN: 978-0-615-26447-9

Edited by: Pamela L. Willard and Shanna Gregor

Printed in the United States of America

CONTENTS

Acknowledgements

David and Gretchen dedicate this book to Jesus, each other, and their children: Georgia, Savannah, Oran, and Truman.

Special Thank You To

Pastors Zane and Jan Anderson
Pastor Eli and Olivia Marez
Pastors Scott and Maureen Stanek
Don Gossett
Pastors Tony and Mary Jackson
Pastor Joan Boethel
Reverend Nancy James
Pastor Scott and Christine Brown
Pastor Carmine Zottoli
Pastor Keith Campbell
Pastors Ken and Sandy Lowry
Pastors Brian and Jocelyn Severin
Dale and Maureen Burke
Stan Moser
Bill Rupert
Konya Ferrell

Special Thank You to Churches

Bastrop Christian Outreach Center - Texas
Faith Bible Church – New York
His Word Ministries – New Jersey
Victory Christian Fellowship - Colorado
Victory Worship Center – Arizona

INTRODUCTION

For all those who desire a new outlook on life, have the courage to achieve it, and embrace the abundant life that God has for you.

THIS book has been an amazing journey. Fourteen months before this book was published, I never realized that a transformation would take place in my heart in regard to my own conflict, balance, and breakthrough. I didn't anticipate how a book can change your life. I had to relive some of the best and worst moments of my life. Time has a way of "smoothing out the bumps" of life and easing the memory of them. In order to accurately recount some of the stories I asked God to bring me back to what happened and how I was feeling. I really wanted to get to the heart of my conflicts as well as my victories. Also, as I wrote I found myself asking, "Do I really believe that? Do I really live it?" The answers to those questions and more are in the pages of this book.

Early on in the process Gretchen came along side me to help write, edit, and put her touch in every chapter. Her duties as a mother and teacher of our four children didn't diminish during her effort. She never wavered in the vision we shared for this book. Like me, she faced questions from her own life that surfaced during the writing process. She recalled the challenges conflict brought to her life, studying her Bible to find balance, and walking together with God for many breakthroughs.

Everywhere you go conflict is there. No matter which way you turn, life isn't always easy. Obstacles seem to block our path and it can get frustrating. Conflict can infiltrate our decisions, relationships, employers, spouse, children, church, and how we view God.

Just when your conflict seems like it is going to overwhelm you, something happens to tip the balance of life in your favor. It could be a good deed by a friend or family member. Perhaps it is the work of our great Savior. As the good balance in your life increases, conflict moves further away and things start to look up. You anticipate it will keep getting better but change is difficult. In order for things to truly revolutionize your life, you realize the need to seize control over your decisions and work toward something beyond mere balance. You start to believe in the success that is in God's heart for you. Your vocabulary becomes different. You set in motion the victory God has for your life.

A breakthrough is headed your way. When you take steps to align your life with the plan of God you become empowered against your previous life of conflict. You realize that nothing can hold you back and a life of victory is at your fingertips. Keep pressing on. Keep pressing in. A mighty God is ready to assist your every step. Live the breakthrough life God wants for you!

CHAPTER 1

CONFLICT

"Many are the afflictions of the righteous: but the LORD delivers him out of them all."

(Psalm 34:19)

CONFLICT may not be our destination of choice but many of us frequent it every day. We never intended to arrive at conflict. We never wanted to stay. But we continue to reside in conflict not knowing how to get out. There are many types of conflict. Simple conflicts happen to us everyday. Conflict can also occur in our mind, will, and emotions. Spiritual conflict is the agenda of Satan. Often overlooked, there is the conflict that we cause in our own life.

You think of different things when you hear the word. Let's simplify it by stating conflict is what keeps you out of balance between your spiritual life, family life, and work life. Conflict is a thief that robs you of peace, distracts you from your goals, and holds you back from many breakthroughs in life. Conflict stifles your chances for victorious relationships. Conflict keeps you from financial balance and monetary freedom. Conflict slows career enhancement, inhibits success, family unity, and the joy God intended us to have throughout our lives. I've realized if you want to overcome conflict, you have to first understand it. As you read on, you will discover how to eliminate conflict from many areas of your life. We need to define conflict to begin our understanding of it.

I am using Webster's 1828 Dictionary because of its historical accuracy regarding biblical Hebrew and Greek words:

Conflict (Noun):

1. Fighting or combat of individuals or armies
2. Contention and strife
3. Struggling with difficulties; a striving to oppose, or overcome.
4. A struggling of the mind; distress; anxiety.
5. Opposition

Life without God = Conflict.

Conflict brings to mind such things as disputes, arguments, troubles, disagreements, or general discord from a personal situation to even actions between nations. Perhaps you have a picture in your mind of one of your own conflicts you faced recently. When conflict arises our minds are void of peace, joy, happiness, tranquility, and thoughts of overcoming. It is a negative and stressful word. Life without God is all conflict.

One Monday morning a few years back, I planned to wake up early to get ahead on my work at the office. By choice, I stayed up too late the previous night watching my favorite show and did not wake up on time. My day started out with time conflict.

Selfishness always brings conflict.

Not desiring to take any personal responsibility, I blamed my alarm clock for my inability to get up. It did not take long to get in a bad mood and I started a contentious argument with my wife. Contention is a form of conflict described in Webster's 1828 Dictionary as strife, struggle, contest, or quarrel. *Proverbs 13:10* states: *"Pride leads to conflict; those who take advice are wise." (NLT)*

The Bible goes further and tells us that strife invites every evil thing into your house. *James 3:14-16* states*: "If you have bitter envying and strife in your hearts, glory not, and lie not against the truth. This wisdom descends not from above, but is earthly, sensual, devilish. For where envying and strife is, there is confusion and every evil work."*

I was already late so I continued my day on a run. I was impatient with my family and yelled at my kids for slowing me down. I do not like to admit it but I was a selfish person for many years of my life. Selfishness always brings conflict. I did have some concern for others, but to be honest with you I was more concerned about how others related back to me.

This was a bad day.

Have you ever met someone who is full of themselves? That was me before Christ—I was full of myself. I was the life of the party, gregarious, and full of energy on the outside. On the inside, I did not consider others feelings or opinions. I thank God for His mercy and my wife for her sweet, open spirit which helped me see things from another's point of view. As much as possible we need to extend mercy and grace to those we have conflict with. We are all on life's journey to become more like Jesus.

I left the house in a hurry and was driving too fast. The roads were icy and I slid off of the road. Somehow, I had not damaged my car and managed to continue on to work. At the commuter train station I had to wait another 45 minutes. I was going to be late for my first meeting that was arranged to resolve a conflict between two employees.

After catching the next train and arriving at my destination, I hustled onto the street. Absorbed in my own impatience and mental conflict, I was nearly hit by a car crossing the street on my way to the front door of my office.

Arriving at the office and having missed my meeting, I noticed the coffee machine was broken so I went to a café nearby to get some coffee. After I ordered, I realized I didn't have my wallet so I was unable to pay.

Angered and full of conflict about my day so far, I uttered an impatient word or two under my breath. Surely it couldn't get any worse.

I was told my position was being eliminated.

Back at my desk for a very late start on the day, angry consultants met me that had not been paid on time. I had enough and met them yell for yell. I then went to my regular weekly meeting with my boss only to be told that my position was being eliminated. After some serious words of conflict with my boss, I was advised to take the rest of the day off to decide if was going to take a severance package or not.

Now my day has gone from bad to horrible. On my way home I waited for more trains before I could get back to my vehicle. Looking in the direction of my parking space, I discovered my vehicle had been stolen from the parking lot. Then I waited for two hours for the police to arrive and take my statement. Amazingly, I managed to hold my tongue and not express my frustration with the police for taking so long.

I called my wife to pick me up. She was really upset and told me that her father was terminally ill from a lung infection that was in conflict with the antibiotics used to treat him.

Following the anguishing call with my wife, my realtor called and told me the pending contract for the sale of our house had fallen apart due to a conflict with the buyer's finances. He suggested we should lower our price and go back to square one.

After my wife arrived to pick me up, the transmission went out in her car and stranded us 3 miles from home. It was too far to walk in the cold so we waited another 2 hours for a tow truck. $500 dollars and a rental car later I was in conflict mentally, physically, financially, spiritually, and emotionally.

All of the above things are true and did happen to me. However, they did not all happen in one day. (whew!) They occurred over a period of years both before I was a Christian and during my walk with the Lord. Perhaps you have experienced some or all of these situations.

My bad day was a multitude of conflict that came from circumstances around me. Some conflict was caused by me. Some conflict was caused by others. Some conflict just happened. How I dealt with all of this conflict was a direct result of my maturity in Christ (or lack thereof). Conflict will come against us. We can prepare for it if we understand how our mind works with our spirit.

Difficulty is conflict.

Please raise your hand if you have ever experienced difficulty. Jesus said *"In the world you will have tribulation; but be of good cheer, I have overcome the world." (John 16:33 NKJV)*

Difficult things are hard, full of labor, and confusing. If you are anything like me, you do not like anything that comes with hard labor and confusion. I like things that are easy, simple, and straight-forward. Difficulty is another definition of conflict. I am really beginning to dislike the word conflict and I hope you are too.

The more conflict you have, the greater the difficulty you will experience in life. It will not stop on its own but only grow to challenge your soul. Conflict can destroy you in spirit, soul, and body if you do not work with God to eliminate it.

CONFLICT

"Many are the afflictions of the righteous: but the LORD delivers him out of them all."

(Psalm 34:19)

Chapter 1 Reflection:

1. How do I define conflict?

_____

_____

_____

_____

2. What conflicts impact my day to day life?

_____

_____

_____

_____

3. How does conflict in my life affect others?

_____

_____

_____

4. Can I relate to "the bad day" story in the chapter?

_____

If yes, which part?

_____

_____

_____

Prayer to repeat out loud:

"Father God thank You for taking me out of conflict according to Psalm 34:19. Your Word says that You deliver me out of all my afflictions. Thank You that I am affliction free. I pray this in the name of Jesus, Amen."

CHAPTER 2

SOUL CONFLICT

"Casting down imaginations and every high thing that exalts itself against the knowledge of God, and bringing into captivity every thought to the obedience of Christ."
(2 Corinthians 10:5)

GOD created your soul: your mind, your will, and your emotions to be a blessing and guide to you.

1. *Is your mind a blessing to you?*
2. *Do you trust your thoughts?*
3. *Can you trust your emotions?*

We are a spirit that lives in a body, and has a soul.

What is your soul? Your soul is your mind, will, and emotions. Let me clarify that we have a mind, a will, and emotions. But, that is not who we are. That is what we have. Moreover, our soul is where conflict occurs. We have a soul and a body but God created us as a spirit. It is our spirit that spends eternity with Christ in heaven. Our body does not. There is no conflict in our spirit because it is purified when we ask Jesus to be our Lord and Savior. *"Therefore if any man be in Christ, he is a new creature: old things are passed away; behold, all things are become new." (2 Corinthians 5:17)* It is us, our spirit that becomes new in Christ. Our body and our soul do not.

Our body is given to us to take care of. It is our lease on life. When our body quits we leave this earth. We cannot exist here without our body. Treat your body with carelessness, and it will not last as long as it should. Our soul is filled with every thought, word, smell, and experience we have ever had; some good and some bad. Our soul needs to be renewed by continual study, prayer, and time with God.

Before we met Christ, it took years to fill our minds (soul) with ungodly thoughts. When we receive Christ, the miracle of salvation immediately cleanses us from all past sin. Often, certain behaviors and habits also are removed from us, but many are not. It took a long time for us to fill our soul and it takes time with God to cleanse it. How much time depends on our commitment to following God. *"Throw off your old sinful nature and your former way of life, which is corrupted by lust and deception. Instead, let the Spirit renew your thoughts and attitudes. Put on your new nature, created to be like God—truly righteous and holy."* (Ephesians 4:22-24 NLT) Our soul is where conflict exists. It takes effort from you to renew it to the things of God.

An unstable thought life is a very real struggle.

When your mind is bombarded with adverse thoughts, emotions, doubt, unbelief, or worry, you cannot function as the whole and entire person God intended you to be. You and I must be keenly aware of mental conflict so that those distressing and anxious thoughts do not get hold of our well-being and affect our health. An unstable thought life is a very real struggle for most people at one time or another. *James 1:8* states *"a double minded man is unstable in all his ways."* (NKJV) Double minded means that we meditate on God at the same time we entertain thoughts that are contrary to the Word of God.

Your mind is the original information super-highway.

Thoughts, ideas, emotions, and words fly around and through

your brain constantly. Information hits you from all angles, from many sources, all the time. The information in your minds can originate from you, others, the devil, or from God. You must work with God to destroy all destructive thoughts and replace them with instructive and enhancing ones. Embrace the good and filter out the bad.

"Casting down imaginations, and every high thing that exalts itself against the knowledge of God, and bringing into captivity every thought to the obedience of Christ."

(2 Corinthians 10:5)

Fill up the highway of your soul with thoughts that help and encourage you. Turn your eyes and ears away from things that hurt you and toward what helps you breakthrough into God's kind of thinking. How do you do it? Like a computer, you start by uploading the Word of God into your mind.

If you make a habit of filling your mind with God's Word, it will flow out in response to any crisis. If your thoughts are on fear and anxiety, that will come out.

Examine the following two scriptures on God's guidance for your thought life.

"Keep this Book of the Law always on your lips; meditate on it day and night, so that you may be careful to do everything written in it. Then you will be prosperous and successful."

(Joshua 1:8 TNIV)

"Finally, brethren, whatever is true, whatever is honorable, whatever is right, whatever is pure, whatever is lovely, whatever is of good repute, if there is any excellence and if anything worthy of praise, dwell on these things."

(Philippians 4:8 NASB)

Now ask yourself these questions:

1. **What do I spend my time thinking about?**
2. **What thoughts enter my mind and do I want to focus on them?**
3. **Do I find myself imagining things that are far away from reality?**
4. **What things can I think about that will actually improve how I think about myself, others, and the world around me?**

We have all heard the saying "garbage in, garbage out". Our minds are full of what we pour into them. The concept is very much like how we treat our bodies. I am sure you have heard, "You are what you eat". If you eat poorly, you may not see the results today, but over time, the results will be inevitable. Our bodies will begin to break down and physical sickness will result. We must care for our bodies for long life and health. Endeavor to create an environment that nurtures your growth in God. You create that environment by meditating on the Bible day and night, as well as thinking on the pure, honorable, and praiseworthy thoughts in life.

Thought Life

Before I was a Christian, I had difficulty with my thought life as well as my emotions. I was angry, impatient, and shared the world's way of thinking. I entertained any thought that entered my brain such as an angry thought to get back at the boss, imaginations at the sight of a pretty girl, or devising ways to get ahead. These thoughts never came to fruition, but they still existed within my brain. I considered them normal and something everyone dealt with. What I did not realize until I discovered God and His ways, is that an unstable thought life always brings conflict. Luke tells us in his gospel that we need to have patience in order to possess our souls. (*Luke 21:19 NKJV*)

If you allow your mind to entertain any radical thought that occurs, you can potentially end up doing anything. Every day thoughts come into the minds of people who choose to lie to get ahead, cheat on their spouse, or simply justify ungodly behavior. Justification of sin, unethical, and immoral activity is easier when we have entertained the ideas in our minds for many months or years. It's like a movie playing in your head and you watch it so many times that you eventually believe it can't be that bad, or you become obsessed with it and carry it out. It is thoughts like these we must cast down and throw out of our mind.

Thoughts become reality.

Have you ever wanted a new car but you knew it wasn't the right time to buy it? Your finances couldn't quite justify it, but you went ahead and bought it anyway. Maybe you had to tighten your belt and things turned out okay, but it probably caused a hardship on you and your family. We have some experience with this.

We had been thinking of getting a new car in anticipation of having children in the near future. The topic was discussed and even narrowed down what type of car we would like. We were in no hurry because both of us had cars that were debt free. One weekend we had some free time so we went to "just look". It didn't take long before we saw the car we had been talking about. Either we convinced ourselves we should get it or the salesman did. Due to our prior meditations on a new car, we had already visualized the purchase in our minds. The result was we drove off in a new car that we didn't need and couldn't really afford.

We made an easy day for our salesperson. We traded in a perfectly good car with no payment, for a payment we could barely manage. Yes, it was ultimately our decision to purchase, but the sales staff involved knew we could not easily pay for the car. Yet, they pursued the sale with great zeal. Everyone in the situation was pursuing self-interest.

That type of self-interest thinking comes with a cost. We had it and the salesman had it. (*Matthew 16:26*) lets us know the cost is nothing less than our soul. *"For what profit is it to a man if he gains the whole world, and loses his own soul? Or what will a man give in exchange for his soul?"* (*NKJV*) What you allow to enter your life will have a direct outcome.

You are never cheated if you are a child of God.

Along with self-interest is a very important concept I like to call "I Am Cheated Syndrome". I Am Cheated Syndrome rears its ugly head wherever and whenever people feel like they might be taken advantage of. Their flesh generally puffs up and defends their right to be right. You see it everywhere you go. People cut off others in traffic, swoop in front of you to get a closer parking spot, cut in line, complain that service takes too long, and so much more. It is the devil that plants thoughts in our head that we are or might be cheated. You are never cheated if you are a child of God. God is for us and not against us. *"If God be for us, who can be against us?" (Romans 8:31)*

The enemy whispers a perception in our ear that we are cheated. When you feel I Am Cheated Syndrome rising on the inside you must reject it. The I Am Cheated Syndrome makes people that suffer from it look foolish.

"How do I know if a thought is from God?"

Through developing my own personal relationship with Jesus Christ, I learned that I do not have to accept every thought that enters my mind. I can rebuke and eliminate the thoughts that do not glorify God. *2 Corinthians 10:5* tells us to *"cast down every argument and every high thing that exalts itself against the knowledge of God and **bring every thought into captivity** to the obedience of Christ." (my emphasis added to show that you can change your thoughts)* You and I have a simple command to capture and throw away all thoughts that are not of God.

You may ask, "How do I know if a thought is from God?" Here is a simple way to check by asking these questions: Is it in agreement with or in opposition to what is in the Bible? Does the thought glorify God? Would my spouse be upset? Is it something I could tell my kids about? Would my mother approve? Depending on your answers, all thoughts can be easily categorized as either for God or against Him.

You also must strengthen your mind by filling it up with the Word of God. You can do that by reading, thinking, and meditating about the Bible day and night as *Joshua 1:8* shows. After you meditate on God's Word His peace will flow in your life and create balance.

My boss wanted me to lie.

When I was a new Christian, I was excited about the things of God and began to let go of my old habits. I no longer wanted a temper, no longer wanted to use foul language, and did not want to participate in conversations about behavior I was trying to change. These past conversations were about parties, drinking, or how to get an advantage at work for a promotion. These are not easy things to do while working for a construction company on a remote jobsite. Some of my co-workers at the time did not understand my new faith and actually increased the pressure on me with louder language, longer hours, and anger towards me. I felt as if my soul was in torment trying to hang on to its old way of thinking compared to the new way I was feeding it.

In fact, my boss wanted me to lie to his wife to help him cover an affair he was having and I refused. I also refused to talk to his wife to ensure I did not get caught in the middle his situation. Because I was constantly renewing my mind through prayer, Bible study, and surrounding myself with other positive Christian influences at church, I began to make decisions based on God's standards, not mine. *"He restores my soul; He leads me in the paths of righteousness For His name's sake." (Psalm 23:3)*

My work situation increased my strain and stress simply because I refused to participate in a hostile work environment like I used to. Everything finally boiled over with a heated argument between me and my boss where he publicly screamed at me. In the intensity of the moment my soul and my mouth forgot all about my desire to not use certain language. The conflict had to do with an issue about where to place cardboard boxes. It sounds trivial and it was. Most arguments are trivial and this was no exception.

I was accused of not moving empty boxes to the correct place. I felt I had no right to be accused, but I also had no right to react with anger. The truth behind the argument was the fact that I was no longer welcome as an employee due to my new faith.

Conflict within the arena of our mind and thoughts is very destructive to our life. You must work with God to renew your mind. All conflict is in opposition to God's great plan for your life. The enemy will be happy to test your faith to try and get you to back up from your journey with God.

SOUL CONFLICT

"Casting down imaginations and every high thing that exalts itself against the knowledge of God, and bringing into captivity every thought to the obedience of Christ."
(2 Corinthians 10:5)

Chapter 2 Reflection:

1. Why is it important to renew my mind to the things of God?

_____

_____

_____

2. How should I renew my mind in order to think God's way?

_____

_____

_____

3. What areas of my life do I need to renew with the Word of
    God?

    _____

    _____

    _____

4. How does conflict in my thought life affect others?

    _____

    _____

    _____

Prayer to repeat out loud:

*"Father God, give me the ability to renew my mind with Your
Word. I submit my thought life to You and Your direction. I thank
You that I have the mind of Christ. I take authority over areas in
my soul that do not glorify You and command them to leave in the
name of Jesus."*

CHAPTER 3

SPIRITUAL CONFLICT

"For our struggle is not against flesh and blood, but against the rulers, against the authorities, against the powers of this dark world and against the spiritual forces of evil in the heavenly realms."

(Ephesians 6:12 NIV)

SPIRITUAL Conflict's roots are based on Satan and his angels falling out of God's plan and presence. His weapons are not found in our physical world but come against us from an unseen dimension. A natural adversary is tangible, but in a spiritual fight, conflict comes from negative thoughts, whispers, suggestions, and ideas. Like God, Satan is a spirit. But Satan cannot alter the natural and physical laws God has set up in this universe and use them against us. Instead, he uses guile, deceit, pride, fear, sickness, and lies against you in his spiritual fight to advance his darkness. His goal is to cause us to be in conflict with God. Conflict is the opposite of peace. The opposite of good is evil. God is the opposite of Satan.

We cannot forget that we have an enemy out there that is constantly trying to trip us up by placing temptation in our midst and causing us to fail. He constantly bombards us with ideas, words, and examples that are contrary to the Word of God. If we do not recognize his ploys of distraction, diversion, and temptation we can be constantly tripped up by his efforts. Where strife abounds, evil has every opportunity *(James 3:16)*. The devil wants conflict. The devil is conflict.

Our hidden foe is often overlooked due to our inability to see him with our natural eyes. If you are a Christian you do not need to fear the unseen but you do need to be aware of it. Satan is real. Hell is real. His demons are real. He wants you to join him at his vacation "hot-spot".

"Our adversary the devil roams about like a roaring lion seeking whom he may devour."

(*1 Peter 5:8*)

Notice in the scripture above that the devil walks around "*like a roaring lion*". Acting like a lion means he imitates the behavior of one. A real lion seeks out the lame and sick to attack. Satan's goal is to prey on our weaknesses and hurt you when you are in need. He attempts to trick you into believing his lies about your life and circumstances.

Satan has no real power but to deceive, lie, and distract us. He wants you separated from the safety of others so that he can stalk you, capture you, and destroy you. He constantly opposes you in life and constantly desires to make your life full of conflict. The good news is that Jesus has defeated him with life bringing love and power.

Know Your Adversary.

Do not be fooled, Satan's ways are subtle. He often speaks a whisper in your ear hoping to plant an idea or a thought. If you accept an idea, whispers come more often and become louder. Over time, if you are not careful, you may do things that seem unimaginable today. For example, no one falls into adultery overnight on a whim. Adultery is conceived in the mind long before a physical manifestation occurs. Listening to the ideas and whispers of the adversary starts a destructive process. Satan's conflict plants unrighteousness if you allow him the opportunity. Knowing your adversary can keep you from disaster.

Satan is the accuser of the brethren.

Satan's only ability to affect our life is to accuse us of wrongdoing and suggest sinful behavior. The Bible calls him "the accuser of the brethren". The brethren are all people that believe in Christ. *Revelations 12:10-11* says:

> "*Then I heard a loud voice in heaven say: "Now have come the salvation and the power and the kingdom of our God, and the authority of His Christ.* **For the accuser of our brothers, who accuses them before our God day and night,** *has been hurled down. They overcame him by the blood of the Lamb and by the word of their testimony; they did not love their lives so much as to shrink from death."* (NIV my emphasis added)

Satan cannot make you do anything. He can only suggest, implicate, and repeat his foul doctrine. He is trying to get you to agree with evil ideas and take them as your own. He is conflict. He is all about conflict and nothing else. If you receive his conflict, he will just increase his lies toward you.

The devil cannot read our mind but he does see our actions and hears our words; be careful what you speak. He learns our weaknesses and will send thoughts to you that focus on what those weaknesses are. For example, if you are easily angered, he will whisper anger filled thoughts in your ear. If you are easily offended, he will whisper offense to you.

Satan will enter in areas of opportunity where you have struggled in the past. If you are insecure about your relationship with Christ he will tell you things like, "You are probably not a Christian. You really aren't a good person. People don't like you. You will never overcome your problems." Thoughts like these are not yours. They come from your enemy and fuel conflict in life. The devil does not give us thoughts we will never agree with. For example, if you have never committed a crime he will not tell you to go rob a bank.

I remember having a conversation with my wife where she said something I didn't agree with. Immediately I received a thought in my head that said, "You should tell her how it is. You don't have to take that."

Now, at that moment I had a choice. I could listen to the thought or cast it down. Where do you think that thought came from? It certainly didn't come from God. That only leaves two choices: It either came from me or from the devil. Either way, the thought did not glorify God so I threw it away. I purposefully replaced it with a thought about how caring and loving my wife is. Just like that, the conflict was solved.

The world is in conflict with God.

Even after we become Christians the adversary works against us. Why? We are members of God's Kingdom of Righteousness. Satan was thrown out for rebellion and disobedience against God himself. He is angered by what he lost and wants us to lose it as well. *"Many are the afflictions of the righteous, but the Lord delivers us from them all,"* (Psalm 34:19) if we just ask. Real life continues to happen as long as we live and breathe on planet earth. The world will always throw its worst at you.

The world promises one thing to all that breathe its air, opposition. In Webster's 1812 Dictionary, opposition is: *"an attempt to check or restrain any effort; resistance, or an obstacle in your path"*. The world's system is not set up to bring peace and harmony. Plus, we have an adversary that only seeks to harm and destroy us. He comes to destroy our lives and everything in it by dividing us away from friends, family, church, and God.

Jesus is our peace.

Jesus said, *"The thief comes to steal, kill and destroy, but I have come to give life and give it more abundantly."* (John 10:10) Overcoming conflict exists in a relationship with the Savior, Jesus. You can have no peace without a belief in Jesus. *Isaiah 9:6* states *"and the government shall be upon His shoulder: and His name shall be called Wonderful, Counselor, the mighty God, the everlasting Father, and the Prince of Peace."* Jesus is our strength, comforter, advocate, and peace. We must rely on Him and not on our own abilities.

"These things I have spoken to you, so that in Me you may have peace."

(John 14:27)

The voice of God must be stronger in us than the whispers of the adversary. God is continually speaking to us with holy, positive, and encouraging thoughts. As you grow in your personal relationship with God, His voice will become familiar to you. In *John 10*, Jesus compares our relationship with God to a sheep following a shepherd. Jesus said:

*"I tell you the truth, the man who does not enter the sheep pen by the gate, but climbs in by some other way, is a thief and a robber. The man who enters by the gate is the shepherd of his sheep. The watchman opens the gate for him, and the sheep listen to his voice. He calls his own sheep by name and leads them out. When he has brought out all his own, he goes on ahead of them, and his sheep follow him because they know his voice. **But they will never follow a stranger; in fact, they will run away from him because they do not recognize a stranger's voice.**" (John 10:1-5 NIV – My emphasis added)*

As we tune our ear to the voice of the Good Shepherd, we'll know what He sounds like every time. Fine tuning your ear comes from spending time in the Word of God, in prayer, and around other Godly influences. If your mind is full of God, when the stranger—the devil—whispers to you, you'll know better than to listen. God intended for you to recognize your adversary and utilize the Word of God to nullify his impact on your life.

Conflict comes, trouble comes, but neither can stay.

Everyone has experienced some type of trouble in his life because we live in a world that does not submit to the goodness of God. God does not bring us trouble but Jesus warned us it would come. Jesus said to be of good cheer because by His strength we can overcome any circumstance that is before us. He has overcome Satan and the wickedness of this world. Jesus said:

> *"In the world you have tribulation, but take courage; I have overcome the world."*
>
> *(John 16:32-33)*

Agreeing with conflict is a choice. If you succumb to Satan's lies and temptations you will end up living in fear. It makes no sense to fear someone that has already been defeated. Fear drains your strength to resist the devil and inhibits your ability to believe God in faith. *"For God has not given us a spirit of fear, but of power and of love and of a sound mind." (2 Timothy 1:7)* If you have fear, you do not have a sound mind.

The devil is not worthy of the slightest bit of credit or attention from us. Jesus defeated death, hell, and the grave with his resurrection from Calvary's cross. Jesus told us in *John 14:6* that *"I am the way, the truth, and the life."* Through Jesus, Satan has been defeated and rendered powerless.

God is love. God's love eliminates all fear as noted in *1 John 4:18,* *"There is no fear in love; but perfect love casts out fear." (NKJV)* When you acknowledge God's love you enter His Kingdom of abundance, health, and joy. Many of us love God but are held back from His fullness by the choices we make. Self-induced conflict is something that we can all overcome.

SPIRITUAL CONFLICT

> **"For our struggle is not against flesh and blood, but against the rulers, against the authorities, against the powers of this dark world and against the spiritual forces of evil in the heavenly realms."**
>
> **(Ephesians 6:13 NIV)**

Chapter 3 Reflection:

1. How long do I listen to negative thoughts when they enter my mind? Why?

    _____

    _____

    _____

2. How can I overcome negative thoughts?

    _____

    _____

    _____

3. Do I believe that Christ alone is enough to overcome spiritual conflict? How?

    _____

    _____

    _____

4.   What areas of my life do I need the peace of God?

_____

_____

_____

Prayer to repeat out loud:

"Father God, I take authority over the enemy's spiritual forces set against me in life. The name of Jesus is above all names and no darkness can prevail against the name of Jesus. I purpose in my mind to rebuke Satan's thoughts. Instead I choose to follow the Prince of Peace. In Jesus name, Amen."

CHAPTER 4

SELF-INDUCED CONFLICT

"Do not be deceived, God is not mocked; for whatever a man sows, that he will also reap."

(Galatians 6:7)

SELF-INDUCED Conflict is conflict you create and develop on your own. Your decisions, or lack thereof, have positive and negative outcomes for nearly every situation in your life. What you say, where you go, who you see, and what you do have far more impact on your life than you may realize. These conflicts can be minimized or even eliminated as you work with God to achieve His plan for your life.

God is there to help guide us and keep us in peace instead of conflict. He promises it throughout His Word if we keep our mind on Him. *"You will keep him in perfect peace, whose mind is stayed on You, because he trusts in You." (Isaiah 26:3 NKJV)* The things we do are up to us. Think about the following two questions: Have you ever asked yourself how much impact you have on your life? Have you accepted the outcomes of your decisions and taken responsibility for them?

Good ideas are not always God ideas

Many years ago my wife and I were friends with a successful single parent who held a good job and provided well for her daughter. She became so singularly minded about serving God and the church that she quit her job with no plan for future income. Certainly no reasonable person would stand up and say that serving God is a bad idea. At the time, it sounded like a spiritual and noble position that many others wished they had the faith and confidence to do. As with most things, there is another side to the story.

God provided that good job and her ability to care for her daughter after a difficult family struggle. Although I do not hear God for other people, it seemed to me very unwise to make such a drastic life-change without a specific plan or direction from the Lord. The decision was made from an idea. That idea was immediately acted on. I do not know if the idea was prayed about or thought about for any length of time. But I have discovered there are many good ideas that are not necessarily God ideas.

For every decision, there is a result.

Unfortunately, this person soon lost her house and car and was left to doing odd jobs to get enough to eat. One decision created an enormous amount of personal conflict. Should God be blamed? God gave her the job in the first place. The strain of her situation continued for many years and the family required regular assistance from church and friends.

That is an example of self-induced conflict. Today's choices will directly reflect our future circumstances. The decisions you make today will specifically provide an outcome in the future. You don't have to be a statistician or a mathematician to work out all the possibilities; you just need to understand that for every action there is a reaction. Whatever things we sow we are sure to reap a harvest from it. Decisions equal results.

> *"Do not be deceived, God is not mocked; for whatever a man sows, that he will also reap."*
>
> *(Galatians 6:7)*

Self-Induced conflict is a simple concept yet can bring serious opposition to our daily lives. No one is perfect nor makes all of the right decisions, but knowing we affect what happens to us in the future should give us pause. Pausing before a decision gives time for praying, thinking, and analyzing our decisions.

Abraham's Conflict

The book of *Genesis, chapters 11-24*, records the life of Abraham. Abram (He was later renamed Abraham meaning "Father of Faith" by God) and his family, resided in the land of his forefathers, Ur of the Chaldees. At the age of 75, God spoke to Abram and called him to move to a far away land that he had never seen called Canaan and promised to make him the father of a great nation. Abram's journey was full of hardship and the entire spectrum of conflict. His soul was in conflict believing the promises of God. Great difficulty came to Abram from self-induced conflict when he had trouble telling the truth to people in authority. Spiritual conflict threatened to destroy a part of his family that was seduced by the wickedness of Sodom. Natural conflicts from famine and battle were a daily threat.

It is likely that his decision to leave was the source of disagreement among friends and family. Imagine leaving everything you have ever experienced, everyone you have ever known, and every place you have ever been. Do you think it is possible that Abram experienced conflict even before he left? People of the past, as today, did not like change. His family, who stayed behind were probably not happy with his decision. While he was personally confident of God telling him to relocate, Abram's family that chose to go may not have been happy with his decision. Whether they wanted to go or not, his wife Sarai and others went with him. *Conflicts with family transpire when differing opinions about life's direction occur.*

After a more than 1,000-mile journey, Abram and his followers experienced a famine. To avoid the conflict of no food, he led his group to Egypt for sustenance. Sarai was very beautiful and upon arrival Abram feared the Pharaoh would attempt to take her as a wife and kill him.

Out of fear, Abram deceived Pharaoh by not telling him Sarai was his wife. His deceit led to a conflict of Pharaoh desiring to wed her. Even though Abram made a faithless decision, God brought plagues to Egypt to protect Sarai and remove her from her potential betrothal conflict. Pharaoh sent Abram and his followers away to avoid more conflict in his kingdom. *When the truth is hidden and deceit is purposefully done, conflict is always the result. Deceit and lies are spiritual conflicts from Satan. Our choice to operate in them is from conflict in our soul and creates self-induced conflict.*

Abraham's Conflict and Promise

After leaving Egypt, Abram settled in God's promised land of Canaan with his family. The land was not large enough for his herds and those of his nephew, Lot. Conflict and strife occurred between their herdsman and they divided the land and separated. To avoid strife, Abram gave Lot his choice of land. Lot pitched his tent in the land of the wicked and sinful city of Sodom. Soon after his arrival, Lot and his family were attacked and kidnapped resulting in the loss of his wealth and land. Abram took his household and rescued Lot and recovered his provisions through armed conflict.

After his rescue Lot returned to the plains of Sodom. Over time, Lot's mind became entrenched in Sodom's evil. His life became a sad example of self-induced conflict as he offered his daughters up for prostitution. His wife disobeyed the Lord and turned into a pillar of salt in the process of escaping the city before God destroyed it. *What we see and experience on a daily basis will enhance or reduce the conflict we experience in life.*

Time progressed and Abram continued in his walk to become the father of the great nation promised by God. Since he was an aged man, the promise seemed impossible. Abram needed to walk out this belief over time until his trust in God's Word built up enough to receive the promise. He and Sarai even tried to help God's plan along by fathering a child from his wife's servant, Hagar. The birth of Ishmael was the result from this relationship occurring outside of God's original plan for Abram. (Abraham's children are still at war to this day in the Middle East.)

After the birth of Ishmael, Sarai despised Hagar and Ishmael and forced Abram to send them away to the desert wilderness never to return. *We invite conflict when we complicate the call and plan of God on our life with impatience and unbelief. God is always working on our behalf. Only conflict can result when we attempt a variation of what God has shown or promised us.*

Creating the image of faith

God needed to rebuild Abram's image of faith in his mind and renamed him Abraham, the father of many nations. With this new name, Abraham's conflict in his mind gave way to the confession he was the father of many nations. God also renamed Sarai to Sarah which means "noble woman" in Hebrew. Soon, the child God promised was born and Sarah became the mother she was promised to be. *Many years of unbelief by both Abraham and Sarah delayed God's promise. The conflicts that occurred in Abraham's life were the direct result of decisions that occurred outside of what God promised.*

Like us, Abraham experienced much conflict but ultimately came to a place of breakthrough and victory when he accepted and walked out God's plan for his life. His own name of Abraham rehearsed and recalled God's promise in his mind until it became more real than his physical circumstances. Abraham is called the Father of Faith in the Bible because he refused to let go of God's promise. He walked out his promise by cultivating his friendship with God. God asks us each to do the same thing today by placing our trust in Him.

Quality decision making

As with Abraham, many of the conflicts and situations we experience in life can be avoided by better decision making. I am not trying to disregard truly unexpected or tragic events that happen from time to time. We live in a fallen world that is not the perfect garden God originally designed for us. Bad things do happen such as natural disaster, war, famine, death, sickness, and economic hardship. But God does not cause these events against us. They are natural processes of this planet, physical limitations, or results of man's lustful desire for power. Those are the events where faith in God, family, and church support must come along side of us.

Allowing room for those unexpected events, the majority of all conflict can be avoided or alleviated by quality decision making. Quality decision making is very important in leading a balanced life. Decisions that are well thought out with both pros and cons considered lead to quality decisions. Decisions are influenced by our ability to submit to God. If you do not consider God in your decision making, the adversary will assist you by suggesting his ideas for your life.

Quality decision making is not a gift that some people have and others do not. It is an ability that we all possess. However, like the muscle in your arm, if you want it to get stronger you have to work it. People with superior abilities did not get that way by sheer luck. Think of an Olympic athlete; it took many years to perfect the skill that makes them a world-class athlete.

Our decision making process works the same way.

1. What do you do when you make a bad decision?
2. Do you repeat it down the road?
3. Do you learn from it so you can avoid a similar situation in the future?

Learning from experience is a valuable way to gain knowledge. However, it is often painful and not the most effective. Associating with others you can trust and learn from is a better way to gain knowledge without having to attend the school of Hard Knocks and learn by experience. Study, discipline, observation, and patience are superb teachers.

The best work-out is to study the Bible. We are called to *"be ready in season and out of season" (2 Timothy 4:2).* Knowing the Bible makes you ready to receive a harvest from God.

But God!

It is true that we reap what we sow but God can intervene and stop us from reaping a dangerous harvest. Even when we make mistakes or invite conflict in our life God can bring us out. *"If God is for us, who can be against us?" (Romans 8:31)* But God! God is always present to lift us up and help us if we ask. Asking God to intervene on our behalf, listening to what He says, and obeying Him will stop the dangerous potential of conflict. God wants to eliminate conflict from our life. Balance is the key and must be understood to walk away from a life of conflict.

SELF-INDUCED CONFLICT

"Do not be deceived, God is not mocked; for whatever a man sows, that he will also reap."

(Galatians 6:7)

Chapter 4 Reflection:

1. Do I pray about my decisions before I make them?

_____

_____

_____

2. Where does my foundation for my decisions come from: Experience? Education? Bible? Other?

_____

_____

_____

3. When I make poor decisions, how do I learn not to repeat them?

_____

_____

_____

4. Do I understand that God can intervene and help me out of conflict? Do I believe it?

_____

_____

_____

Prayer to repeat out loud:

"Father God, thank You for helping me recognize where my decisions increase self-induced conflict in my life. I know that what I sow I will also reap. I repent for sowing conflict into my life and give it to You. I thank You for a harvest of victory by showing me ways to overcome conflict in my life. In Jesus Name, Amen"

CHAPTER 5

BALANCE

"A thousand may fall at your side, And ten thousand at your right hand; But it shall not come near you."
(Psalm 91:7 NKJV)

BALANCE is your choice to step away from areas of conflict in your life. A change in direction should be your immediate goal when the storms of life blow against you. *As Psalm 91:7* notes above, balance is a place of stability and refuge. You are in the middle of God's protection.

Webster's 1828 dictionary defines balance:

1. Suspended exactly in the middle, precisely equal weight.
2. Figuratively, an impartial state of the mind.

Balance is when we are holding or juggling all of life's responsibilities with nothing hitting the ground. Balance is the state of mind where we are not angry or happy. It is a situation where we hang on to just enough so we do not fall over or fail. Balance is the point at which we function in life without great success yet have no failure.

Yes, you can function in life yet have no real success or failure. Your career is good enough to keep your bills paid and once in a while enables you to do something you enjoy. But having your bills paid with a small amount of leisure cash is not a long term plan for life's success. It is just enough.

What about your family? You may not regularly fight with your spouse yet you do not really enjoy your marriage. You spend time together but it is never quite as good as it could be. Your children may be home yet all doing their own thing like listening to music or playing video games. No one is upset or fighting; you are just not connected. There is very little family "together" time. You are in balance yet unfulfilled.

Picture an Olympic gymnast on the balance beam. The competitive width of a balance beam is only 4 inches wide. If the gymnast does not have superb balance, the law of gravity will take over in the situation and down she goes. Those with great balance can run, flip, do handstands, twist, dance, and much more on that narrow beam. Gymnasts with poor balance do not even attempt the balance beam; it just becomes a good way to get hurt. In fact, a gymnast with poor balance generally does not stay a gymnast.

We must be consistent in order to achieve balance.

"Therefore, my beloved brethren, be steadfast, immovable, always abounding in the work of the Lord, knowing that your labor is not in vain in the Lord."

(1 Corinthians 15:58 *NKJV*)

For a number of years we enrolled our children in gymnastics classes. To train young athletes in gaining comfort on the balance beam the training starts small. Children are introduced to a beam that is only six inches off of the ground. Young gymnasts practice and hone their "balance" skills with the safety of the cushioned floor only inches away. A mistake only causes a small step down. Even at the low elevation it takes significant practice to stay on that little beam. In order to move up to a beam that is at the competitive height of four feet, five inches off of the ground; balance must be learned and learned well.

Balance: Focus on what is out in front.

Of course like any good dad, if the kids do it so can I. For fun, I attempted to simply walk across the balance beam (the one six inches off of the ground). I hate to admit it but it took me two tries to get across without having to step on the ground to "regain" my balance.

Consider your life and all of the responsibilities and situations you are involved in. How do you get everything related to those responsibilities and situations done? Do you get it all done? If you cannot, how do you prioritize? What do you eliminate? Like the Olympic gymnast, those with good balance generally can get most things accomplished. How is your balance? Do you run and flip without falling? Or, do you expertly operate with the law of gravity and have it all come crashing down?

Many spend years leaning too far to either side, falling down, and having to pick up the pieces. Our lives grow heavy with the burden of doubt, worry, anxiety and all of the conflict that accompanies these words. We then build complicated habits or methods for dealing with the fact we are leaning too far to one side just to stay up. For example, we may work long hours and we reason it is for the good of the family. We may drive too fast but it is to get home faster. Achieving balance by excuse is not really balance. It is conflict.

I realized a great truth in my attempt to cross the balance beam. Our lives are similar. If we lean too far away from what we are able to handle, we fall off and drop something. *Proverbs 3:6* showcases how to balance, *"In all your ways acknowledge Him, and He will make your paths straight."* *(NIV)* Jesus is our balance beam. If we focus on Him and His ways, our path will not waver to the left and right. He makes our paths straight.

Submitting to Christ

If we go about our daily life thinking everything is just fine when it really isn't; we deny the reality of our situation. Unfortunately, denial can only temporarily hold back the wave of truth that always arrives. To achieve a balanced life, we must submit the will of our life to the plan of

Christ. Submitting to His plan involves our recognition that we cannot make all of our decisions on our own. We must acknowledge that our past decisions did not always produce the best results. Basically, we must give in to the fact we need assistance. God is waiting for us to ask for His help.

What do we do when we are out of balance? We may join a small group to talk about our problems. Or, we might buy the latest technology in an attempt to become more efficient. We buy a faster car to arrive on time or stay at work later to get everything done. We ignore the rest of the world and go to a quiet place just to take a breath.

Running from or avoiding the truth in life does not change the facts. We must confront the things that send us out of balance and be honest about how we inherited them before we can get rid of them. If you do not know, ask God. He will answer because He enjoys conversation with His children and He wants us whole.

Where we spend our time always ends up being our priority.

If we evaluate what takes up the majority of time and begin to concentrate on the things we value as important in life, we can succeed. What are your priorities? Where you spend your time always ends up being your priority. What do you do with your time?

Your time priorities are critical if you want to achieve balance in your life. *"Where your treasure is, there also is your heart." (Matthew 6:21 NKJV)* In this scripture, substitute your "time" for the word "treasure". If you work 70 hours per week, work is your priority. It is not because you have to work that much; it is generally because you want to or do not know how to balance other areas of your life. If you spend a lot of time on hobbies but your house is a mess, hobbies are more important to you than a clean house. The areas and ways you spend your time show what is important.

What distinguishes a good choice from a bad choice?

With all the choices you make in your life, some will be good and some will be bad. I've made many of both, and many in between. What distinguishes a good choice from a bad choice? Well, that all depends on individual circumstances and point of view. What is a good choice for me may be a bad choice for you.

For example, I choose to live in Tucson, Arizona. Although I have lived in many places across the United States, I like Arizona best. In fact, as an Arizona native I love everything about Arizona: the climate, the sunshine, the scenery, and even the cactus (unless I get too close). Alternatively, someone born and raised in northern Idaho may truly dislike Arizona. He may think it is too hot, may dislike the flora or fauna, and may be easily sunburned. Do these things make Arizona a bad place to live? Well you already know that the answer is; depends who is asking.

There are choices that are bad for every one no matter what they are. Taking drugs or drinking large amounts of alcohol is bad for all of us. Eating ten pounds of fried bacon per day will generally raise blood cholesterol. (Sorry if I burst your bubble on that one.) Staring at the sun will cause eye damage. Driving too fast will result in tickets and higher car insurance. Basically, excessive amounts of most things are bad for you. Don't forget, this is the section about maintaining balance.

Many struggles are balance and choice issues.

People rarely complain about the good in life, just the bad. Many go through life complaining about the things that happen to them. God deals fairly with all men and desires all men understand Him. Matthew 5:45 demonstrates this principle: *"that you may be sons of your Father in heaven; for He makes His sun rise on the evil and on the good, and sends rain on the just and on the unjust."* (NKJV)

It is true that in certain circumstances, bad things do happen to good people and the truly unforeseen events make life difficult. However, the majority of other things in life are a direct result of choices we have made in life that have made us out of balance. Many of the things we struggle with on a daily basis are balance and choice issues.

I have had several speeding tickets in my life because I chose to drive too fast. I really did not think I was driving too fast but the officer did. I willfully chose to go faster than the posted speed limit. On the other hand, I chose to court my wife. She chose to say yes to marriage. Together, we chose to work for many years to make a better marriage. We eliminated conflict and distractions and the result is a marriage we greatly enjoy today. It was no accident, but purposeful, determined, hard work.

When I was just starting out my career in business, I was also starting a new family. It was very difficult to balance the responsibilities of the job with the needs at home. There was a new baby and my wife needed help. I had no idea how much to work or contribute at home.

I had daily questions such as: How long should I stay at work? Is the boss watching the clock? Will I get in trouble if I actually leave on time? How are my wife and the baby? What should I do? What is more important?

The answers are different for you than they were for me—each situation is uniquely different. God can and will meet us in the middle of our decision making and give us the wisdom to choose what brings balance in our life.

"If any of you lacks wisdom, let him ask of God, who gives to all liberally and without reproach, and it will be given to him."
(James 1:5 NKJV)

Although I certainly tried to always make good decisions, I did not always do so through the years. Sometimes, it takes experience and the passage of time to figure out where our balance lies. It is important to learn from the opportunities that we have gone through in order to repeat the good and reject the bad. God can help. *"I have set before you*

*life and death, blessing and cursing; therefore **choose life**, that both you and your descendants may live." (Deuteronomy 30:19 NKJV- my emphasis added)*
Choose life means to choose what is best for you, your family, and others according to God's Word. All we need to do is to ask God for help. In the midst of our indecision or times of strife He is with us to help us make the right choice. God is always with us.

"I will never leave thee, nor forsake thee."

(Hebrew 13:5)

Remember, life takes time.

Everything we do in life has a direct result in not allowing us to do something else. For example, if you go to the grocery store you cannot go to the ballpark at the same time. If you go to sleep you cannot be awake. If you go swimming you cannot go running at the same time. If you love someone you cannot hate them at the same time (no matter what you may "feel" like.)

Read the following questions. It is important to understand what you do shows what you think is important. What you do not do shows what you consider to be less important. How do you balance it out?

Questions: Remember, Answer Honestly!

1. *How much time do you spend watching TV per day?*
2. *How much time do you spend on the internet?*
3. *How late do you stay up?*
4. *How early do you get up?*
5. *How many extra-curricular things are on your plate?*
6. *Do you choose to study the Bible?*
7. *Are you continually working on your life to become a better person?*
8. *Do you consider those around you before making a decision?*

People will invent any variety of reasons why it is ok or not ok to do certain things. Any behavior can be justified. Any bad deed can find a friendly audience and all good acts can be repeated. The world around us is a product of everyone in it as well as those that have lived before us. It is the balanced product of all their choices, both good and bad. You are a product of your environment and a balance of all the choices made before you. Yet, you always have a choice.

The love of God is what enables us to overcome and succeed. *"The love of God has been poured out in our hearts by the Holy Spirit."* *(Romans 5:5 NKJV)* God's love also created the universe in perfect balance. God is the great equalizer. God shows His commitment to balance with all of creation. The earth is balanced perfectly in the solar system. If it was further away it would be too cold. If it was closer it would be too hot. The sun emits the perfect amount of heat to sustain life on earth. Our atmosphere is made of the perfect equalization of oxygen and nitrogen. If the mixture was in different proportions, our atmosphere would not sustain life.

Balance comes by the love of God.

He also created you and me to be in balance. God desires that we live a life of balance. Creation is not out of balance and neither should we be a pendulum that swings from one extreme to another. He created us to walk in His ways and His Spirit. Walking in God's Spirit brings balance into our life.

> *"This I say then, Walk in the Spirit, and ye shall not fulfill the lust of the flesh."*
>
> *(Galatians 5:16)*

So how exactly do you walk in the Spirit? The answer comes one step at a time. One brick must lie upon another before any large construction project is completed. You and I are a construction project that needs a strong foundation and strong layer upon strong layer. Walking in the Spirit is not difficult, but does require action on our part such as:

1. Contemplating the promises and parables that exist in the Word of God and what they mean to your life are other building blocks.

2. Worshiping the Lord with the praise of your heart. *"Speak to one another with psalms, hymns and spiritual songs. Sing and make music in your heart to the Lord." (Ephesians 5:19 NIV)*

   a. Worshiping brings you closer to God and unifies your heart with His. A heart of worship walks in the spirit. *"True worshipers will worship the Father in spirit and truth, for they are the kind of worshipers the Father seeks." (John 4:23 NIV)*

3. Associating with people who are full of life and integrity can help show you some of God's simple truth regarding how to live.

4. Developing daily prayer is essential to continually strengthen your life to walk in the Spirit.

5. Spending time with the Creator by reading the Bible and thinking about His promises for your life is the beginning of walking in the Spirit.

Speaking to God or speaking His Word is what prayer is.

As you study the Bible you must also speak it out in prayer for change to impact your life. Speaking scripture and its positive, Godly words protect your soul from conflict and bring balance. *"By faith we understand that the worlds were framed by the Word of God, so that the things which are seen were not made of things which are visible." (Hebrews 11:3 NKJV)* Just as the worlds were framed by God's Word, our personal world is framed by what we say. If you aren't sure what to say, say words of blessing and encouragement. *"Pleasant words are like a honeycomb, Sweetness to the soul and health to the bones."* *(Proverbs 16:24 NKJV)* Prayer and pleasant words brings balance.

Speaking to God or speaking His Word is what prayer is. Prayer, simply put, is a conversation with God. As we speak to Him, God will protect us as noted in Philippians: *"Be careful for nothing; but in every thing by prayer and supplication with thanksgiving let your requests be made known unto God. And the peace of God, which passeth all understanding, shall keep your hearts and minds through Christ Jesus."* *(Philippians 4:6-7).* When we bring our concerns and conflicts to God, He in turn passes His peace to us. God's peace of mind will remove conflict. When conflict leaves, balance takes its place.

Prayer creates balance in life and brings answers to many questions. *"The effective, fervent prayer of a righteous man avails much."* *(James 5:16 NKJV)* In Christ, we are all made righteous. Our prayers are righteous in God's ears. His answers are help for us to overcome life's daily challenges.

Prayer is not a one-way, boring repetition from us to God, but a dynamic, lively conversation between a loving father and His children. Prayer bursts with life and empowers the soul. I, for one, cannot make it through one day without talking to my best friend in prayer.

The entire reason for Jesus' death on the cross was to restore our relationship with the father. *"For everyone who asks receives, and he who seeks finds, and to him who knocks it will be opened."* *(Matthew 7:8 NKJV)* God is earnestly seeking some time with us in an intimate way through our conversation with Him.

Prayer does not have to be fancy. You do not need to sound like a theologian with all of the right words. All you need to do is talk to God like you talk to a friend. What is important is to approach prayer with an open mind and a sensitive heart. Prayer with pure motivations is the most powerful force on earth. God responds to simple, heartfelt prayer.

What do you say to God? Try something simple like this. "Here I am God, what do you want to talk about? I am listening." Or, "God, let me tell you about my day." He will respond. He is compelled to respond. Just a simple talk is all He asks.

Remember, just because we can hang on to our circumstance or situation does not mean we should. Balance is stability but to achieve breakthrough we need to step beyond it. Stepping beyond to the breakthrough takes Godly choices.

BALANCE

"A thousand may fall at your side, And ten thousand at your right hand; But it shall not come near you."

(Psalm 91:7 NKJV)

Chapter 5 Reflection:

1. Do I struggle balancing too many items in my life?

    _____

    a. If yes, what items are not really necessary for me, my family, and my overall happiness?

        _____

        _____

        _____

2. What are some things I can do to simplify my life?

    _____

    _____

    _____

3. Are there areas that I know I am out of the will of God? What are they?

_____

_____

_____

    a. What can I do to change these areas?

_____

_____

_____

Prayer to repeat out loud:

"Father God, thank You for revealing the perfect balance in my life. I thank You that I recognize things in my life that do not glorify You and help me in removing them. Thank You for showing me how to not only achieve balance but push past it to overcome my circumstances and my situations. In Jesus name, Amen."

CHAPTER 6

CHOICES

As every man hath received the gift, even so minister the same one to another, as good stewards of the manifold grace of God."

(1 Peter 4:10)

EVERY day is filled with choices. It starts with choosing to get up, eat, brush your teeth, and continues all day. Most of the choices you and I make are conscious decisions about what to do, or not to do. As the scripture above explains, God has freely given His gift of love to each of us. All we need to do is make a choice.

Absolute truth only comes from God.

The world thinks that if a decision doesn't physically hurt anyone or cause pain and suffering it must be ok. There will never be agreement on right and wrong in the world because it has no absolute truth from which to base decisions. Absolute truth only comes from God. It does not come from higher education, philosophy, politics, or religion. That's right. I said religion. Religion is a system where man creates rules to fence God into an easily understandable box. God did not invent religion, man did. All God wants is a relationship with you so He can give you His understanding and friendship.

As man invented religion, man also invented the economic and political rat-race we all live in. The "rat-race" was not invented by God but by rats. How can we expect to excel at something only a rat is good at? To run around in chasing unattainable goals at the expense of our family, integrity, and health is not worth it. A typical person caught in the rat-race of life will end up exhausted and frustrated. I say we leave it to the rats and go a different direction with better choices.

Real Life is full of choices.

Have you ever seen a mini-van with those little window stickers on the back window depicting dad, mom, kids, dogs, and the cat? They are certainly cute and exude family commitment. Those pictures tell everyone that the owner is unashamed to advertise that there is a whole bunch of people in that van. Sometimes, there is even an honor student among the group from so-and-so elementary. Those are the families to watch out for.

Actually, there is nothing wrong with these window stickers. As a father of four, it makes me shudder to think of all the things those parents must do to care for and transport their entire crew around. Does dad or mom belong to any social or business clubs? Does either parent help coach or assist in after school activities? Are there activities that require the parents to be in seven places at once? Is mom involved in a school group? Are the kids in sports? Does the dog go to the dog park? Does the cat have any friends? Does the cat care about anything?

If you say yes to everything, prepare yourself for some conflict.

Any or all of the above questions could have a yes answer. All those yes choices have one thing in common. They all take time. A lack of time related to poor time management is one of the leading causes of conflict. If you say yes to everything, prepare yourself for some conflict and a very limited control over your time.

If we really want to gain control and direction in our lives, we must honestly understand the different things that take up our time.

Where do we choose to spend our time? What or whom do you serve? *"Choose for yourselves this day whom you will serve?" (Joshua 24:15 NKJV).* It varies from person to person and it really is up to us.

Everything we do takes time whether we like it or not. Going to the park or playing golf takes a few hours. It also takes a few hours to clean the garage or wash the car. Which do you enjoy more? It really depends on our point of view. When analyzing choices, we must consider the potential items that we give up every time we choose to do something specific.

In order to get a clear picture of where you choose to spend your time, make a simple chart of your daily and weekly activities. As accountants say, the numbers do not lie. Below is a generic day for me. As a self-employed individual, my day may be different than yours as far as work time and priority. Just because you like to do it, does not mean it has a higher priority or takes less time.

Activity	Estimated Time	Priority
Bible study	1 hour	High
Family time	2 hours	High
Check email	30 Minutes	Medium
Return phone calls	30 Minutes	High
Work on client items	7 hours	High
Help with school	1 hour	High
Clean office	30 minutes	Low
Go to store	1 hour	Low
Go to bank	30 minutes	Medium
Go to business meeting	2 hours	High
Sweep porch	30 minutes	Medium
Go to park with kids	1 hour	High
Lunch	1 hour	Very High
Walk dog	1 hour	Medium
Do dishes	30 minutes	High

Every day is a balance between schedule and what must be done.

If you add all the hours up I have a 20 hour day! No thanks on that. So, what goes away? What choices do I have? Every day I must balance what is scheduled to occur, with what must be done. Additionally, some things just cannot be cut out for me such as Bible study, time with the kids, and certain client work that is on a deadline. Things like golf, car wash, bank, store, porch, and maybe even certain emails or phone calls can wait. Remember, you control your schedule. You will experience many breakthroughs in time and prioritization when you understand your schedule does not control you—you control your schedule.

Other people, circumstances, or commitments controlling your schedule cause conflict.

When you allow other people, circumstances, or commitments control of your schedule you reap stress and conflict. It is understandable that your employer or place of work controls your schedule for certain hours of each day. Your attitude within that allotment is up to you. Do you choose to enjoy your work? Do you give it your all? Do you get by with drudgery and complaining? It really does matter when we attempt to gain control over our time.

I have given much thought to what should stay and what should go within my day. I do not like to spend time doing things that do not benefit my family or others in some way. I try to make wise use of my time but it is often difficult. By no means is my list comprehensive of all the things that I may or may not do in a typical day. It is just an example to get you thinking about all of the things that are in your schedule and the priority they have.

There are good results or bad consequences to every choice.

Most of the items on our schedules were put there by the person you look at in the mirror each day. That person is you. So, let's think about this. If I am almost always out of time and I put all of the things on my schedule, then I am to blame, and I am the one who can fix it. Now we are on the right track. What are you choosing to do that you really do not want to? What are you not choosing to do that you would really like to be doing?

There are good or bad consequences to every choice that we make. If we make the wrong choice, the price for that choice is paid by ourselves and others. Today we live in an age where there is serious lack of personal responsibility. When people make mistakes they often cast blame away from themselves. It occurs up and down the socio-economic spectrum; from politicians, to Hollywood actors, to business leaders, to you and to me. It always seems to be someone else's fault. No one else should answer for your choices.

The result of a choice

When I was 20 years old, two friends and I went up to the mountains of Arizona to go skiing. I did not have any money so I sold my history textbook to raise the funds for ski rental and lift ticket. I planned to share a book with another classmate to finish the class. We were young and careless and really did not think about the consequences of our actions the day before our ski trip.

The night before our trip all three of us were out late with friends. 3:00 am was the departure time to leave for the 5-hour drive up to the mountains. On very little sleep, we made the drive up a very windy mountain road and skied all day. We had arranged to stay with a friend that lived nearby but at the last minute decided to head back to our college dorm rooms. *It was our choice. No one made it for us.*

We were all very tired after exerting ourselves all day on very little sleep. We agreed to keep each other awake with conversation, but the car was warm and we were exhausted. Barely 30 miles away from the ski resort my friend John, who was a passenger fell asleep. A few minutes later I fell asleep. Immediately after I dozed off, Stephen, the driver, went to sleep too. At nearly 70 miles an hour our vehicle veered off of the road down a rugged embankment, crashed through trees, flipped over, and landed upside down in the bottom of a ravine.

Stephen and John were ejected from the vehicle and since I was in the middle of the pickup, I was thrown to the floor and pinned inside. I remember some loud crashes and some moaning as I struggled to regain consciousness. As my mind cleared I realized I was in incredible pain in my back, head, and arm. I had hit my head on the dash during the crash and had a severe concussion. My right arm was pinned underneath the vehicle and could not move. It hurt so much I was not sure I still had a hand because I could not see it under the metal. My back seared in pain with torn ligaments and a broken vertebra in my lower back.

God is always with us. He is for us, not against us. All the time.

All the time I could hear deep rasping moans from my friend John somewhere beyond me in the dark. Fear gripped me! Fear like I had never felt in all my life, before or since. I panicked and started screaming uncontrollably.

Stephen was also severely hurt with a deep head gash and from smashing into the steering wheel. He managed to climb the hill to get help. In my panic I heard him yell to calm down and that help was coming. Somehow the authority in his voice snapped me out of my confusion and I began think about what I needed to do. All I could think was to pray, "Lord please don't let us die and please don't let me be paralyzed."

I was not a Christian then but I felt a peace come over me and I started to get out of the vehicle. I managed to dig in the soil under the vehicle to free my trapped arm. Amazingly it was not broken—I didn't even have a scratch. In a few minutes the pain left as my circulation was restored. I managed to inch my way out of the vehicle and lay very still, thrilled I could still wiggle my toes. We experienced many miracles in the next few hours.

Upon reaching the highway up the hillside, Stephen managed to flag down several vehicles. The first car that stopped was driven by an emergency medical technician (EMT), our next miracle. He immediately assessed the situation and attended to John who was in very bad shape. John had four broken ribs that had punctured his lung causing it to collapse and bleed internally.

The next car that stopped had a vehicle cell phone which was not common in the early 1990's – another miracle. Based on the EMT's assessment of our condition a helicopter and ambulance were immediately dispatched to our location. Many people continued to stop and supply emergency first aid. Some even prayed for us for healing and recovery. I truly believe that angels were in our midst and divine intervention saved us all.

Was our choice worth it?

John was taken by helicopter to the nearest medical facility while Steven and I were immobilized and ambulanced. After five agonizing hours on a back-board, they found that my spinal cord was not in jeopardy and my cracked vertebrae would heal on its own with time. Stephen and I were released from the hospital the next day. John would spend the next 5 weeks in an Intensive Care Trauma Unit. Today we are all 100% recovered from our injuries – another miracle from God. But the experience has never left my mind.

Our choices that day nearly cost us all our lives because we didn't consider how our decision might affect our family, friends, or ourselves. We just acted on impulse. We did what we wanted to do when we wanted to do it. As college students, we decided to go skiing on a whim because we were not accountable to anyone. Nothing was further than the truth. Though we did not know God, we were still accountable to Him. We were accountable to each other and we chose to go. We made the choice to stay up all night. We decided to drive back when we were exhausted. We put ourselves in a position for disaster and we accomplished it.

I know that beyond any doubt that God saved my life and the lives of my friends. *"Look to Me, and be saved, All you ends of the earth! For I am God, and there is no other." (Isaiah 45:22 NKJV)* In my darkest hour I cried out to God and he answered even though I didn't understand or know Him yet. It would be a few more years until I knew him as my personal Lord and Savior.

Consider your choices before you make them.

God saved us by His mercy and grace. He chose to draw close to us even though we did not draw close to Him. He chose to pursue us and save us. God sent His son to die for us so we didn't have to. God is there to help us in every decision and in all circumstance.

"Choose this day whom you will serve."
(Joshua 24:15 NKJV)

Consider your choices before you make them. Other people are always involved in the outcome of your choices whether you think they are or not. How will they be impacted? How do you feel when others try to make your choices for you?

Convenience or Inconvenience?

I remember when I was a teenager, my dad was busy fixing something on his old Jeep when the phone rang (back then, phones actually rang...) "Hey Dad, the phone is ringing, are you going to get it?"

My father matter-of-factly answered, "No, I am busy. Whoever it is will just have to be patient. *Their convenience cannot be inconvenient for me right now.* " There it is; convenience should not be inconvenient. That really stuck with me though the years. Although I have not always followed his advice, when things get really crazy, my father's words ring in my ears. This is especially true with today's dependency on cell phones. Why am I always inconveniencing myself or my family for a circumstance or distraction that is not as important as what I am doing? It sounds crazy, but we do it all the time. Thanks Dad.

The small things really do count.

How you choose to do the smallest of things will determine how you act on the largest of stages. Our choices are all equally important. It doesn't matter if they seem insignificant. Balancing all of the outcomes of a choice and what its potential impact can become leads to break-through planning and thinking. God cares greatly about every choice.

"Thou hast been faithful over a few things, I will make Thee ruler over many things."
(Matthew 25:21)

If we are not careful, our lives will be spent dealing with unnecessary people, money, or time issues. Good choices must occur in our most basic decisions. The little things really do count. They certainly matter to God and they absolutely matter to us.

Like you, I have been guilty of saying yes to everything that came along. Believe it or not, saying yes to many items in life brings forth conflict. Many times I have tried to cram too much into one day and accomplished far less than anticipated. Because I am a true optimist, I think I can do it all. I also think that way of everyone around me.

Yes, to volunteering. Yes, to be on this committee. Yes, to another meeting. Yes, I will take that phone call. Yes, I can stay a little late. Yes, I would love to go here. Yes, I can go there. Yes, I can go bonkers because I have too much to do. No one can do it all and no one should try. Nor should we expect it of others.

A little bit of no goes a long way.

We must exercise restraint and our ability to say no. Saying no in the correct way will help us bring our life into balance. One of the first words for all our children was the word no. From the very start they began to exercise their ability to eliminate unwanted things in their life. That is sort of ironic at the age of one. How do they know what they want? Yet somehow they do. We can say no at age one, but seem to slowly lose that ability as we get older due to peer pressure, family pressure, or work pressure. Remember, Jesus said we must be as a little child. Learn to say no and regain some balance and control over your time.

Saying no, will keep us out of situations we have no business being in. It will keep us from breaking the law, from arguing, from overeating, from staying up too late, from getting up too early, it will keep us away from people that are up to no good, it will keep us off of the internet late at night, it will keep us from losing our temper, and the list goes on. Think about the areas of your life that lack control. A little bit of no goes a long way.

A little bit of no is a key ingredient to achieving breakthrough.

"The prudent see danger and take refuge, but the simple keep going and suffer for it."

(Proverbs 27:12)

Be careful. Saying no is a way of protecting ourselves from being out of balance. However, it is not an excuse to be rude or not fulfill our commitments. If we committed, we must ensure we honor our word and learn to say no in the future. Of course, it depends on what the situation is. If a circumstance is unhealthy, unwise, or dangerous, the most powerful two letter world in the world must be enacted. You must evaluate what you agree to do before starting an action or activity.

In fact, watching my children say no was a big step in my own realization that I did not have to be involved in everything. Saying no "strategically" will actually build your strength and character. Others will begin to see where your priorities are and adjust their requests accordingly.

To make a change in life you start at the root.

How do we put the most important priority at the very top? For most of us, making a large change to the priorities in our life would be distracting and very uncomfortable. We do not like change. People like to know what is going to happen before it happens. With God's help you can put events in life in their proper order.

God is all about change for us. He can help you make a 180 degree turn away from what you used to do. If you were headed east all it takes is to turn around and head west.

For each who wants to make a change, consider this. It took more than an instant, a day, one week, one month, or even one year to get where you are in life. It took many years, many experiences, and many choices along the way to come to the position or situation you find your-self in today. It will take some time to recover and repair the choices that were made along the way. The key is to make good decisions from today forward and ask God for His help to repair anything from the past.

Start at the root. The largest and strongest redwood in the world still started out as a small seed in the beginning. Over time, it grew to become a giant among trees. Your life is like that seed. Changing all of your daily, weekly, monthly, and yearly decisions happens on a small scale everyday. You planted seed to get where you are today. Dig up the bad seeds and water the good seeds. When you spend time in the Word of God, you will learn to plant new seeds in your life.

Jesus tells a similar story in regard to a small seed. *"The kingdom of heaven is like a mustard seed, which a man took and sowed in his field, which indeed is the least of all the seeds; but when it is grown it is greater than the herbs and becomes a tree, so that the birds of the air come and nest in its branches." (Matthew 13:31 NKJV)* Everything large started out as a seed. A seed can be an action, an idea, or a choice. Any one can blossom into something larger than what you started with.

Saying no to the wrong things begins success.

If your boss asks you to do something within your job description and within all the rules of employment, it is a bad idea to say no to your commitment to your employer. Always say no with respect. Do not say no just for the sake of saying it because it can be habit forming. In other words, say no selectively to make your actions in life more effective and efficient.

Saying no to the wrong things is potentially huge for success in life. However, it will not get you past balance into the breakthrough. Saying yes to the right things is what will lead you to a breakthrough in time management. The right things are what bring us closer to God, to our family, to our unique definition of success, and decisions that build and assist others.

Saying yes to the right things leads to breakthrough.

Saying yes to the correct things is what will empower us to overcome our circumstances and situations. Yes is the most powerful three letter word in the world and one of the best positive affirmations that exists. Here are some simple practice ideas:

- ✔ Say yes to more time with family.
- ✔ Say yes to take someone to lunch.
- ✔ Say yes to reading the Bible.
- ✔ Say yes to volunteer your free time to help others.
- ✔ Say yes to pray more.
- ✔ Say yes to eat the right foods.
- ✔ Say yes to tithing
- ✔ Say yes to going to church.
- ✔ Say yes to restore a broken relationship.

✔ Say yes to the right thing when no one else is looking.

Saying yes to the right things is where breakthrough occurs. We must say no to the wrong and yes to the right. No more complication is necessary; keep it simple. Individually, each of us knows what we should say yes or no to. We don't need other people to tell us. Become friends with the Holy Spirit and let Him guide your decision making to a life of breakthrough.

Changing the most basic of decisions such as where to go, who to be with, where to work, what to say, and what not to say is something you can work on every day. You will not always make the right calls. You will make mistakes. It is ok. If you focus on quality decision making, your life will start to tip away from the chaos previously experienced to a more balanced and fulfilled life. Consider your ways and methods in all things before you act. You can make amazing improvements if you stop and think before you act.

Here is your big chance to take the microscope and spotlight off of yourself and shine it on those around you. When you consider others more highly than yourself it turns the key to the door of living a break-through life. Choose to smile at the clerk at the grocery store. Choose to speak kindly to your family. Choose to go the extra mile at work. Choose to drive the speed limit and obey traffic laws. Choose to walk in love. Walking in love promotes breakthroughs in every area of life. Love conquers all.

Walking in love made a huge difference in my life. It took me away from being self-centered. I started paying attention to the little things in life like what I said and did. I soon realized the little things are really important in impacting others in a positive way.

Integrity: The right thing all the time.

When I go to the grocery store, I make a point to put the cart back in the cart return. Why? It is the right thing to do. Is that walking in love? I believe it is. When in its proper place, my cart cannot be in the way of another parking spot and it won't roll off into another person's car. God taught me that walking in love begins with considering others in all of the small things we do on a daily basis.

> *"Be kindly affectionate one to another with brotherly love; in honour preferring one another."*
>
> *(Romans 12:10)*

We have all wished to change the world for the better, improve our city, country or planet. While I am a big fan of all these concepts, on a global scale it seems rather impossible and completely overwhelming. From politicians to pageant winners, the world should have been changed for the better several thousand times by now if they could do what they had promised. The words are easy, but words without a plan are just words. Let's help our fellow man with choices that reach beyond our personal lives.

Breakthrough comes by choosing to walk in the love of Christ.

Only you can influence all of your daily decisions. You are the one who meets and greets many people each day. There are people in your life that I will never meet. There are people in my life that you will never meet. However, if we both choose to do the right things towards the people we come into contact with, something miraculous happens; many people are affected by change. Your change and my change together is a lot of change. We change the world one person at a time. We change the world by walking in the love of Christ. Breakthrough occurs in choosing to walk in the love of Christ.

> *"And walk in love, as Christ also hath loved us, and hath given Himself for us an offering and a sacrifice to God for a sweet-smelling savour."*
>
> *(Ephesians 5:2)*

> *"I call heaven and earth to record this day against you, that I have set before you life and death, blessing and cursing: therefore **choose life**, that both thou and thy seed may live."*
>
> *(Deuteronomy 30:19- my emphasis added)*

Choose to be the example you want to see in your daily life. If you notice something needs changing for the better, you must step in and make a positive difference. If God gives us the desire or the awareness about something, he also provides the grace and ability to help us change it.

God is a gentleman to all mankind.

Let's review one of the greatest choices in human history where the fate of mankind was in the balance between good and evil. In the Garden of Gethsemane Jesus was in great mental, physical, and spiritual agony as the choice to go to the cross lay before Him. He asked the Father if there was another way; a different alternative. His flesh, His mind, and His emotions tore at the very fabric of His being; telling Him not to go to the cross; to avoid certain death and evade absolute agony. Satan sent every available evil thought he could muster to distract and dissolve Jesus' willpower to keep Him from the redemptive path that lay ahead.

> *"And He said, "Abba, Father, all things are possible for You. Take this cup away from Me; nevertheless, **not what I will, but what You will**."*
>
> *(Mark 14:36 NKJV - My emphasis added to highlight that we all have decisions to make.)*

Jesus had spent His entire life on Earth disciplining His body, soul, and mind to listen and obey the voice of Father God. At the end of His earthly life (and the beginning of a restored relationship with God for all of mankind), Jesus stood with the fate of humanity in His hands and chose to follow His destiny as Savior. **He made the choice to go to the cross so we would not have to.** "*God demonstrates His own love toward us, in that while we were still sinners, Christ died for us.*" (Romans 5:8 NKJV)

His selfless and amazing decision has reverberated throughout history and will continue to do so until the end of time. He spent years preparing for His destiny so He could make the right choice for victory when opposition occurred. His historic choice enables you to have choices today.

God is a gentleman to all mankind. He does not force His will upon us nor does He create destruction against us. He leads us, He prompts us, and He has written His Word for us to follow. But the decision to serve Him, or not, is ours alone. Serving God is the ultimate choice and the ultimate breakthrough one can experience. "*As for me and my house, we will serve the LORD.*" (Joshua 24:15)

It is a very important choice; in fact, your very life hangs in the balance. The Bible says that when one of us believes in Jesus for salvation, all of heaven rejoices with us. Go beyond the conflict. Go beyond the ordinary. Take your thinking the next level with the mind of Christ.

Choices

> "*As every man hath received the gift, even so minister the same one to another, as good stewards of the manifold grace of God.*"
>
> **(1 Peter 4:10)**

Chapter 6 Reflection:

1. Do I prioritize what is important in my day-to-day activities?

_____

_____

2. What choices in my day do I need to change?

_____

_____

_____

3. How do others beyond my control impact my choices?

_____

_____

_____

4. Am I ready to choose life and accomplish what I need to do?

_____

_____

_____

Prayer to repeat out loud:

"Father God, thank You for Your guidance regarding my choices and schedule. Thank You for Your love, understanding, and wisdom that enables me to make right choices for the path You have me on. Thank You that Your love enables me to continually seek You. Transform my life into Your great vision for me and all of my family. In Jesus name, Amen"

CHAPTER 7

CHRIST-MINDED

We have the mind of Christ.

(2 Corinthians 2:16)

HAVING **the mind of Christ** should be the goal of every Christian. It is what is missing from those who do not know Him as friend and Savior. The Bible talks about having the mind of Christ. I am sure many have wondered, "What exactly is the mind of Christ?" Simply put, it is the ability to think, analyze, and make decisions the way Jesus did. Remember, those wristbands from the mid 1990's: What Would Jesus Do - WWJD? It is important that we include Christ in all of our decisions. Having WWJD as a reminder keeps me focused on God, His ways, and His methods. We need to think like Jesus in all activities.

Thinking like Jesus is especially important if we do not know what we would do in a given situation. What-Would-We-Do: WWWD? "What Would We Do" will not sell much merchandise because what we do without the mind of Christ is make a lot of mistakes. No one wants to be reminded of past failures. "We" cannot succeed without Christ and His wisdom. His wisdom is always there for us to utilize if we choose to accept it. *"He will never leave us nor forsake us." (Hebrews 13:5)* But we often ignore His mind and only decide with our own.

As we let go of our desire to control all of our decisions and trust in the Lord, our life will become less complicated and more simplified in a way that only God can do. He guides us, guards us, and calls us to be in a relationship with Him. *"The Lord has appeared of old to me, saying: "Yes, I have loved you with an everlasting love; Therefore with lovingkindness I have drawn you." (Jeremiah 31:3)* The love of God is constantly pursuing us. Accepting that His love is given to assist us is the first step in gaining the mind of Christ. What we do in our own ability pales in comparison to what we can accomplish with God.

My wisdom is not enough.

I tend to lean toward the analytical side of things. With formal training in business and an aptitude to tackle problems, I often get caught up with finding solutions in my own strength. I often forget to ask the Lord what He would have me do and charge ahead. Not including the Lord in my decisions creates and stretches out problems.

Years ago I purchased a new car that I thought was great for our family. It was safe, comfortable, and supposedly durable. I did not ask God for his wisdom in purchasing that specific vehicle. After about six months I discovered that the car had issues. At first they were small, from a fuse going out in the radio to a power seat malfunction. Soon the problems escalated into a broken computer core, cracked axle, and a defective transmission. All of these problems occurred before 25,000 miles. Not only were the problems inconvenient, they put us in dangerous situations.

Insert God into the equation.

The problems were all fixed under warranty, but the car was in the shop more than it was with us. After so many issues, I invited God to help me find a new one. My invitation was simple, "Lord, please help me find the right car for us. Make it obvious." With His help, we found a superb car that we drove maintenance free for many years and sold it for a great price when it was time for another.

God not only provides the answer, He is the answer. He represents absolute truth and He would never deceive us. *"God is not a man that He should lie." (Numbers 23:19)* Before embarking on any decision, small or large, insert God into the equation. See what His Word says about your issue or situation. Does Scripture agree with your solution? If not, don't do it.

Some specifics may not be answered in Scripture. If it isn't, you need to ask God in prayer. He always provides one of three answers. Yes, no, or not now. It is the "not now" waiting I do not enjoy. However, the patience learned from waiting is some of the most fruitful growth for understanding the mind of Christ. God's patience gives us the opportunity to check our motivations against His desires for our life. Often when we wait, time solves the decision. Patience is one of God's gifts to us.

God's way of thinking is on a higher level than our own. *"For My thoughts are not your thoughts, nor are your ways My ways," says the LORD." (Isaiah 55:8)* What are His thoughts toward us? *Psalm 139:17* says *"His thoughts towards us are precious."* Psalm 40:5 says God's thoughts about us *"are more than can be numbered."*

Balance occurs by acknowledging God.

Balance comes from committing your problems, fears, and concerns to prayer. Most issues have a way of working themselves out through prayer. All issues are solved when we do what God asks us to do. Prayer has a balancing effect on our life and eliminates conflict. Your success rate over issues will go up dramatically if you do not rush your decision-making process. Pray about it. Think about it. Sleep on it. A good night of sleep helps everyone come up with better solutions. Making decisions when you are tired, distracted, angry, or uninformed will lead to bad decisions. When your mind is alert it hears Christ better than when exhausted.

Balance comes in thinking like Jesus.

It is very difficult to have balance without God in your life.

Everything is confusing without God because His moral compass is not guiding us, ours is. The problem with our moral compass is that we all have a different one. We judge others by their actions and we judge ourselves by our intents. Without the Creator with all the answers, there is no absolute truth or authority from which to base decisions.

The "right thing" with man's wisdom is often the cause of great distress for many because mankind's wisdom is only based on experience and emotion. Yet, many refuse to entertain there is a higher way of thinking already established for us. *"The fool hath said in his heart, there is no God." (Psalm 14:1)* I guess that means God doesn't want us to be stupid. I can't say it simpler than that.

Balance comes when we begin to think like Jesus. We find balance when we renew our minds to the things of God and faith in Christ. The mind of Christ comes through the study of His Word and the contemplation of what it says. We can only do that if we find out who He is and what He is. Only you can change your mind to think the way Jesus' mind thinks. When your mind is renewed toward Jesus you will start to think like Him. *"And be not conformed to this world: but be ye transformed by the renewing of your mind, that ye may prove what is that good, and acceptable, and perfect, will of God." (Romans 12:2)*

Characteristics of the Mind of Christ

In order to think like Jesus you have to take on his personality traits. Jesus was in complete fellowship with the Holy Spirit and shared His qualities. *"The fruit of the Spirit is love, joy, peace, patience, kindness, goodness, faithfulness, gentleness and self-control." (Galatians 5:22-23 NIV).* The Fruits of the Spirit all flow together. Renewing your mind to think like Jesus means integrating the characteristics of each fruit into your thinking.

To think in love is powerful. God so loved the world that He gave Jesus' life for you *(John 3:16).* Are you willing to sacrifice your priorities for the sake of putting others first? Thinking in love enables you to be considerate and kind to everyone you meet. Loving others takes a joyful spirit.

Not everyone is easy to get along with. People make mistakes and do the wrong things. Thinking with joy enables you to look past the deeds of others without becoming upset by their actions. *"The joy of the Lord is your strength." (Nehemiah 8:10)* A peaceful mind creates patience in life.

The Bible says to *"let patience have her perfect work, that ye may be perfect and entire, wanting nothing." (James 1:4)* Serenity in the storms of life gives you stability and power in any circumstance. Patience enables you to take the time you need to sort through your choices in life. The more time you take to pray and keep your mind on God's choices the better your outcome will be. Good outcomes in life make it easy for you to be kind to people because you want to set an example for them.

Having the mind of Christ trains you to be kind to everyone. There is never a reason to fight for your rights against others. God is faithful to defend those that serve Him. God's is faithful to all *(Psalm 89:1)* which demonstrates His commitment to you. When you understand that God is faithful, you become faithful to the people and responsibilities in your life. Faithfulness grows good stewardship over what God has given you. When you think like God, you ensure you are gentle with what He has given you and ensure it is treated well.

The Fruits of the Spirit represent the mind of Christ. As you grow in your ability to walk in each fruit your discipline and self-control will strengthen. You will not be swayed by your adversary and you will have confidence in what God says about you. Not only will you think like Jesus but with you will start to become like Him.

Breakthrough comes in acting like Jesus.

Breakthrough comes when we start to do what Jesus does and act the way Jesus does. We then will fulfill the "WWJD – What Would Jesus Do" scenario because what Jesus would do is what we will start to do. When we start to act like Jesus our life will enter into breakthrough.

Gaining the mind of Christ comes by hearing, saying, and thinking the Word of God. *"Faith comes by hearing and hearing by the Word of God."* *(Romans 10:17 NKJV)* Following Jesus example in faith teaches us how to walk in the will of God.

> *"Don't just listen to God's word. You must do what it says. Otherwise, you are only fooling yourselves."*
>
> *(James 1:22 NLT)*

Here it is on a practical level. Don't just read or listen to the Word of God; do what it says. Think about the happiest people you know. Why are they happy? What makes them different? Is it money? No, even if they had no money they would still be happy. Are they lucky? No, there is no such thing as luck when it comes to happiness. So, what is it?

The happiest people I know are the ones who have their priorities straight. They do not waste time with unimportant details or life's clutter. They have a relationship with God and volunteer their time helping others in some capacity. Yes, it is about giving. *"And remember the words of the Lord Jesus, that He said, It is more blessed to give than to receive."* *(Acts 20:35 NKJV)* Continued breakthrough exists in giving to others. Giving to others can produce a breakthrough in every area of conflict. Serving others with your time, talent, and treasure is where blessing awaits.

> *"Give, and you will receive. Your gift will return to you in full— pressed down, shaken together to make room for more, running over, and poured into your lap. The amount you give will determine the amount you get back."*
>
> *(Luke 6:38 NLT)*

When Jesus physically walked on the earth He spent the majority of His time going around calling people "friend," even when He knew the people He was talking to despised Him. Yet, His attitude made all the difference. Some of those who hated Him became His friend. Yet, those that chose to reject Him were still considered a friend by Jesus. He did not let their attitude affect His. Even on the cross Jesus was busy forgiving His enemies by giving His love.

It is time to give.

When the storms and trouble blow against us and it seems that all hell is breaking loose in our lives, it is time to give. What do we give? Jesus only asks for a willing heart. True service comes from your heart. It means giving your time, your talent, and your treasure where God instructs you. Often, it does not take much to fill a basic need of another person. Can you give simple friendship? Can you give a kind word of encouragement? Can you meet the grocery needs of a family? What does your heart tell you?

As you come across the needs of another ask yourself this question: Can I meet the need? If yes, then how? If not, why? It could be that your finances do not allow it. Perhaps you did not want to. You need to understand the intents of your heart in order to translate them into actions that change your life.

When we take the microscope off of us and put the spotlight on the needs of others, our needs do not seem so important. Thinking of others with the mind of Christ truly gives us a perspective to understand and consider those around us.

Christ did it for you. He put your needs ahead of His own in order to give you His blessings and abundance. The writer of Hebrews says it best, *"Let us consider how we may spur one another on toward love and good deeds." (Hebrews 10:24 NIV)*

We are called to push one another toward love and good deeds. How can you change the world? The answer is simple: one good deed toward one person at a time. That is what Jesus would do.

Christ-Minded

"We have the mind of Christ."

(2 Corinthians 2:16)

Chapter 7 Reflection:

1. When trouble comes my way, what is my first thought?

   _____

   _____

   _____

2. Do I have the mind of Christ? What are its characteristics?

   _____

   _____

   _____

3. Define serving others:

   _____

   _____

   _____

4. What areas do I need more balance and breakthrough with my giving and receiving?

   _____

   _____

   _____

Prayer to repeat out loud:

"Father God, thank You that I have the mind of Christ. Thank You that my mind is continually renewed to the things of God and I began to think and act the way Jesus acts. Thank You that I say what Jesus says and I speak life giving words over everyone I meet. In Jesus name, Amen."

CHAPTER 8

BREAKTHROUGH

"The lord has broken through my enemies like the break-through of waters!"

(2 Samuel 5:20 NASB)

BREAKTHROUGH is where we want to be with every circumstance in life. The previous chapters brought us eye-opening
realizations regarding conflict and balance. The grip of conflict has been
revealed as powerless as we understand the control we can exercise in
changing our life. Transforming our decisions to God's way of thinking
is an enormous step necessary to balance our lives. We are now ready
to explore new understanding and gain every blessing that awaits us.
Conflict and balance are part of the process because we cannot know
where we are going if we are not sure where we have been.

It is time to choose your destiny. It is time to live in the fullness that
God has given us. Living the blessed life is yours for the taking. It is time
for a breakthrough.

What is a breakthrough?

A breakthrough is a sudden, bursting forth event. It is a smashing
through of an obstacle or a mindset that previously existed. Breakthrough
is liberation from captivity in your mind or circumstances. For example,
one minute a woman is pregnant and a breakthrough moment later, she
is holding her baby in her arms.

You experience breakthrough every time you overcome a situation or circumstance that previously seemed difficult or impossible. Breakthrough is not merely gaining hope in a hopeless situation, this is balance. It is the power and ability to overcome the situation. A breakthrough does not just repair a circumstance it removes it.

It takes all the strength and ability God has given you to overcome the difficult situations in life. Our desire for change combined with God's amazing grace and ability are what power a breakthrough in your life.

What does a breakthrough look like?

Breakthroughs are full of power and might. A dam holds back an immense lake. The millions of gallons of water that are behind the lake represent an enormous amount of potential energy waiting to be released. Normally, that energy is transformed into electricity by hydro-electric turbines inside the dam. However, under abnormal circumstances that dam might break and unleash all the raw power of the lake behind it creating an unstoppable wave of energy. That is a great example of a breakthrough.

You are a breakthrough just waiting to happen.

Your life is full of potential energy from breakthroughs just waiting to happen. There are numerous gifts, talents, and abilities inside of you waiting to be unleashed. The Creator bestowed wonderful uniqueness inside each of you for your benefit and to enhance the lives of people in the world around you.

The Berlin Wall for decades after World War II separated the cities of East and West Berlin. It was the "Iron Curtain" in which freedom and prosperity remained just out of reach for those behind it. The strongholds of Communism began to weaken and destabilize throughout the 1980's. A new air of choice began to stir in the Soviet Union.

Citizens hungered for a life without bondage and dreamed of having basic, modern conveniences. Political leaders took notice on both sides of the wall and something amazing occurred. In 1989, after a few pieces of the wall were removed by some very brave people, multitudes joined in and the entire wall was cast down into a mighty heap of rubble. For the first time in decades people were free to come and go after bursting through this mighty barrier.

God is no stranger to breakthroughs.

Joshua led the children of Israel to possess their promised land. Immediately, a large conflict called Jericho stood in their path. Jericho was a huge fortified city with impassable walls. Faced with this seemingly insurmountable conflict, Joshua sought the Lord in prayer. The Lord's breakthrough came in a command to obedience and faith. God asked them to do something that seemed childish and irrelevant.

There was no natural reason why marching around the city in silence for seven days should conquer the wall. In faith, the children of Israel did as instructed by the Lord. On the seventh day, they lifted their voice in a mighty shout of agreement and victory. Their breakthrough occurred in watching the walls of Jericho come down in a pile of rock in one mighty instant by the power of God. *"By faith the walls of Jericho fell down after they were encircled for seven days." (Hebrews 11:30 NKJV)*

Walls of any type cannot stand.

The Berlin Wall and the Walls of Jericho don't just represent a physical breakthrough but a spiritual one. God wants to tear down all the walls in your life. We build walls to protect ourselves but what they really do is hinder us from breaking through into the person God created us to be. People are held captive by the walls of insecurity, fear, doubt, and anger that lay before them. A slavery and bondage mindset dominates how they think and how they view themselves. When these walls come down the possibilities to dream and achieve are opened. Old ideas are thrown away and new life is embraced.

Breakthrough can part the sea.

God demonstrates his miraculous change throughout the Bible. The children of Israel were held in bondage for four hundred years in Egypt in conflict under the oppression and torture of Pharaoh. Balance came when Moses demanded their freedom and they left with the health of God and the wealth of Egypt as compensation for their mistreatment. *"He brought them forth also with silver and gold: and there was not one feeble person among their tribes." (Psalm 105:37)*

After their departure Pharaoh desired revenge and trapped the Israelites on the shore of the Red Sea ready to destroy them but the Lord commanded Moses to lift his staff toward the Sea. *"Then Moses stretched out his hand over the sea; and the LORD caused the sea to go back by a strong east wind all that night, and made the sea into dry land, and the waters were divided. So the children of Israel went into the midst of the sea on the dry ground, and the waters were a wall to them on their right hand and on their left." (Exodus 14:21-22 NKJV)* The conflict of slavery was left behind. On their escape from Pharaoh and the bondage of Egypt, the power of God broke through the Red Sea before Moses and the Israelites went on to freedom. Like the Israelites, many breakthroughs are achieved by walking through, over, and around the walls that surround you.

History's greatest breakthrough

Jesus lived a sinless life and went to the cross for you and me to be forgiven. His conflict was mighty. He was mocked, ridiculed, beaten, tortured, and denied by all. The fate of all mankind balanced in His hands as he took the nails and was put on the cross. Jesus did not call out for help in His final moments of destiny. His blood was poured out for the remission of sin and to restore right relationship with us to father God. In the greatest breakthrough of all, Jesus rose from the dead and rolled away the grave stone of death.

"There was a violent earthquake, for an angel of the Lord came down from heaven and, going to the tomb, rolled back the stone and sat on it.

His appearance was like lightning, and His clothes were white as snow." (*Matthew 28:2-3*) In this breakthrough God saved us from death.

Jesus was tortured and crucified to redeem mankind's sin. He *"broke-through"* and conquered death, hell, and the grave as God's ultimate gift to us. *"I am He who lives, and was dead, and behold, I am alive forevermore. Amen. And I have the keys of Hades and of Death." (Revelation 1:18)*

All of Satan's scheming and evil plans were eliminated in an instance. Sin was destroyed. Death was destroyed. Mankind's rightful relationship with God was restored by the precious blood of Christ. Jesus resurrection proved God's total and ultimate victory.

In Christ

Because of Jesus' sacrifice, you have the keys to a life of breakthrough. He promised that *"He that believeth on me, the works that I do shall he do also; and greater works than these shall he do." (John 14:12)* Jesus gave His ability to all believers. God's grace through the death of Jesus enables everyone to regain relationship with the Father. Since the fall of man in the Garden there has never been a greater breakthrough in all of history. When you choose to give your life to Christ you become "in Christ". His sacrifice moved us into God's kingdom. In God's kingdom there is only breakthrough. *"For the law of the Spirit of life in Christ Jesus hath made me free from the law of sin and death." (Romans 8:2)*

All that Christ is He freely gives to you. His victory over sin and circumstance is yours. *"In all these things we are more than conquerors through Him that loved us." (Romans 8:37)* To ensure you understand you are a child of God in His kingdom *Romans 8:37* clearly says "more" than conquerors. Being more than a conqueror means not only overcoming your situations but aligning your life with Christ against the adversary in victory.

God's Grace is important in a breakthrough.

Alignment with God against Satan ensures your ability to surmount any obstacle. *"I can do all things through Christ which strengthens me." (Philippians 4:13 NKJV)* His power helps us overcome by His grace.

Grace is a key element in a breakthrough and can be defined as God's unmerited favor; but it is also His power, willingness and ability to help us do what we cannot do on our own. It enables us to do what He has called us to do. *"And the Word became flesh and dwelt among us, and we beheld His glory, the glory as of the only begotten of the Father, full of **grace** and truth." (John 1:14 – my emphasis added)*

God's grace is breakthrough power for you.

Strong's Biblical Concordance defines the original Greek meaning of the word *grace* in this verse. *"Charis"*, pronounced (khä'-r s), is defined as God's *"good will, loving-kindness, favour a) of the merciful kindness by which God, exerting His holy influence upon souls, turns them to Christ, keeps, strengthens, increases them in Christian faith, knowledge, affection, and kindles them to the exercise of the Christian virtues"*

Grace is a power word. It is God's power word. We need all we can get. God is *"exerting His holy influence upon our souls and turns them toward Christ."* Often we attempt to change, succeed, or overcome by our own will, ability, and strength. When we do this we usually fall short or fail in some way.

Consider a time where you mentally formulated a plan to accomplish something. In order to meet the goal you exerted willpower and energy to change and adjust circumstances during the process to achieve that goal.

It is even possible that certain facts were omitted or added to ensure the goal could happen without all of the proper buy-in. It is exhausting to try and hit targets by mental effort and physical exertion. Not accomplishing a goal might be considered a failure to some but accomplishing a goal through manipulation or deceit is a certain failure in God's eyes. God's methods are better and come with the power and ability to achieve.

I know in my own life my biggest struggles were always in situations where I tried to solve things by myself. In my own power and will, those struggles turned into the hardest challenges of my life. For most of my adult life I have struggled with relying on my reason to solve problems for me and my family. For example, there have been seasons in our life where we wondered if we had enough money to pay the bills. I was always trying to figure out what bill to cut out or how to earn more income. I cannot recall ever having peace about either one of my approaches.

When I turned my situation over to God, He always made a way for us to prosper. I cannot fully explain it in natural terms. It is supernatural. When we submit to God, he meets all of our need. *And my God shall supply all your need according to His riches in glory by Christ Jesus." (Philippians 4:19 NKJV)* When I turn to God for His help the issues before me go away. His grace, peace, power, love, wisdom, guidance, and deliverance are all sufficient compared to the solutions I can work out in my brain.

Jesus wants and needs us to live in His blessing and overflow.

If we accept God's grace in our life by choosing to believe His Word, reading it, and spending time with Him; His ability helps us overcome and achieve by the power of the Holy Spirit. *"For our gospel did not come to you in word only, but also in power, and in the Holy Spirit and in much assurance." (1 Thessalonians 1:5 NKJV).* The Holy Spirit is our helper in time of need and accomplishes God's work through people on earth. Jesus explained the Holy Spirit this way, *"But the Helper, the Holy Spirit, whom the Father will send in My name, He will teach you all things, and bring to your remembrance all things that I said to you." (John 14:26 NKJV).* If we deny God's grace and the Holy Spirit's help in our life by trying to do things without God, we open the door to Satan and his negative influences.

Jesus wants us to live in the blessing and overflow. As we are blessed, we can bless others around us. God never wanted His church broken, discouraged, lost, confused, and weak. God wants His church healthy and victorious.

God wants us whole, peaceful and complete with nothing missing, broken, and everything working. *"For I know the plans I have for you," declares the LORD, "plans to prosper you and not to harm you, plans to give you hope and a future." (Jeremiah 29:11 NIV)* Can you imagine a life like that? God imagines it for us everyday. All we need to do is agree with Him and realize that conflict cannot defeat us.

A large part of our victory is how we react.

Even in the most troubled times where life has struck us a mighty blow God is still with us. We live in a fallen world with fallen people needing salvation. People that do not know Christ as Savior do not make great choices. People can hurt or be hurt by others. Trouble can also come from this fallen world, like disaster or disease. I know people that have overcome cancer and ones that have lost the battle for life to cancer. I know people that had wealth one year and declared bankruptcy the next. Like I said, we live in a fallen world. It was not God's original plan for us to live with difficulty. He intended us to have a perfect world with no sin but Adam brought death through his disobedience.

You may ask what does this have to do with the blessing and break-through? Very simply, God loves all people and it is only in God that we can have victory. God is always directing us toward His peace, healing, and power. A large part of our victory is not what happens to us but what we choose to do about it and how we react. His grace is always with us and when we acknowledge it, it surrounds us. When we ask for His help it overtakes us, goes beyond us and eliminates the obstacles we haven't even experienced that lay before us. God's grace provides us with many unconditional gifts. They have already been given to us and our job is to open them. God is waiting for us to do so and receive His fruits. *"But the fruit of the Spirit is love, joy, peace, longsuffering, kindness, goodness, faithfulness, gentleness, self-control." (Galatians 5:22-23 NKJV)*

No one else on earth acts like, thinks like, or looks just like you. We are unique individuals created in the image of God. Every person on earth is part of His master plan. When God creates something He calls it good. When He looks at His children, He understands we are good. It can be no other way from His point of view. When He says something, He means it. God's plans for you are good. His gifts are yours every day for the rest of your life. God does not bestow gifts on you only to remove them later. They are yours to keep. *"For the gifts and calling of God are without repentance." (Romans 11:29)* God always tells the truth to you. *"God is not a man so He does not lie." (Numbers 23:19 NLT)*

The breakthrough happens when you "let go and let God" invade your life and give you His specific direction. You must operate with Him, not without Him. The world today is full of advice, opinions, and quick fixes. I am not against any of those things. But if you let those things take the place of God in your life you miss the point.

Breakthrough is where we need to be living all day, every day.

Look at the world around you. Does it seem like people are waiting for someone to help them? Do they want someone to show them a successful way to live? Are you an example they can follow? Or do you need to find someone to follow who can build your confidence and help give you a successful point of view? How you think about God, yourself, and others indicates whether or not you are ready for a breakthrough or if you're going to remain stuck with more of the same issues.

> *"Be not conformed to this world; but be transformed by the renewing of your mind, that you may prove what is that good, and acceptable, and perfect will of God."*
>
> *(Romans 12:2)*

I wanted to find people that were living a blessed life.

When I was a new Christian, I sought out people who had walked in faith for a long time and that were living a blessed life. I had enough experience with the "unblessed" life full of challenge and difficulty. I knew there was a better way to follow the road drawn by others so I would not have to spend years learning how to live. I wanted to emulate and copy the good things that were observed. My wife and I found a few key individuals that we could learn from. We watched their marriage, their conversation, their children, their countenance, their character, and their relationship with God.

One of our examples was a couple that had served as missionaries overseas. They had a great marriage, super kids, and were always smiling. They were older than we were and had more experience with life and walking as Christians. We spent time with them just so we could learn how they did it. We asked questions and observed how they interacted. At the foundation of it all was their love for Christ and their respect for each other.

Follow the road drawn by others.

We were able to utilize much of what we witnessed to improve our relationship, communication, parenting, and overall spiritual maturity. We learned what to do better, what not to do, and where we stood on solid footing. People are not the standard; Christ is the standard. But people on this earth are here to serve as His hands and feet in creating a better world for us all. I am very grateful to those who helped guide us.

> "Imitate those who through faith and patience inherit the promises." (Hebrews 6:12 NKJV)

I thank God for sending them into our life and giving us the grace to listen. I pray that we can now pass on what they taught us and serve as an example for others. That is how God's promises work. To this day I still seek out the best qualities of everyone I meet and try to incorporate those characteristics into my life. I want to imitate the God qualities I see in other people.

What God says is where true importance exists.

Jesus said true Christianity is not serving self but serving Him and others. Do not be fooled by what the world says is important. Live what you think and know are important to you, your family, and those around you. Set your sights on what becomes eternal.

Breakthrough exists for every part of your life. It empowers you to have a loving relationship with God through a commitment to Christ. It enables you to enjoy every minute with your spouse and children. Breakthrough makes you look forward to going to work and having fulfilling relationships. It infiltrates your finances and your time. It brings the joy of victory to your house.

Victory beckons. With God we overcome every challenge. Be determined and press forward. You can do it. *"I press on toward the goal to win the prize for which God has called me heavenward in Christ Jesus." (Philippians 3:14 TNIV)*

BREAKTHROUGH

"The lord has broken through my enemies like the breakthrough of waters!"

(2 Samuel 5:20 NASB)

Chapter 8 Reflection:

1. What does breakthrough mean to me?

_____

_____

_____

2. What areas in my life need a breakthrough?

_____

_____

_____

3. Do I really believe that God will tear down my walls?

_____

_____

_____

4. What holds me back from trusting God to help me through circumstances?

_____

_____

_____

Prayer to repeat out loud:

"Lord, thank You for a breakthrough in my life. I repent for my unbelief in You and the promises You have for my life. I receive Your total and complete forgiveness and dedicate the rest of my life to working with You to achieve the goals You have for my life. In Jesus name Amen"

CHAPTER 9

GOD

"I am Alpha and Omega, the beginning and the ending, says the Lord, which is, and which was, and which is to come."

(Revelation 1:8)

God. I am that I am.

HOW do we answer the call of God on our life? Everyone who is not a Christian is at conflict with God but God is not at conflict with them. He pursues us with an everlasting love and desires a relationship with us.

Adam was the first person ever created. He and God "hung out" all the time in the cool of the day. They were friends; best friends in one accord. When Eve was created, all three of them were the perfect team of God and humanity.

When Adam and Eve chose to disobey God, they put their will before His will for their lives. Satan deviously put choices before them, but he had no authority to make them choose one way or another. They made a willful choice to disobey. God had explained His rules and the boundaries were set. The fall of man from the garden was no accident. The fall demonstrates that man is prone to make willful choices that are not always in our best interest. Because God loves us, He gave us the free will to choose our path in life.

Understanding past decisions empowers you to change them.

Have you ever wondered why God asked Adam *"Where are you?"* in *Genesis 3:9*? It was not because God did not know what happened or where Adam and Eve were hiding. God asked the question because Adam needed to know where he was.

Adam needed to be confronted with his current state of mind and his recent actions. Adam knew God understood what had occurred. He just needed to admit what had happened and be honest with God. But, instead of immediately revealing their mistake, he blamed Eve in *Genesis 3:12. "The woman You put here with me—she gave me some fruit from the tree, and I ate it." (NIV)* Blaming others for our bad decisions reflects poorly on us. God wanted Adam to take accountability for what happened. Instead, Adam tried to avoid blame and the entire situation.

The Bible is very clear that God is not fooled by anything we say or do. *"Do not be deceived, God is not mocked; for whatever a man sows, that he will also reap." (Galatians 6:7 NKJV)* If we do not come to terms with where our decisions have brought us in life, we cannot move past them.

Adam and Eve were at conflict with God at the fall from the Garden of Eden. Their actions immediately started God's plan to restore our relationship with Him. Jesus is the breakthrough victory at the end of God's restorative plan for humanity.

Competing wills

Every time your will competes with the will of God you are in conflict. It can be over something that is seemingly small such as eating some forbidden fruit. Or it can range to large purchases or life changing decisions about family and career. It really does not matter what elevates your will above God's, only that you have done so. Finding God's will for your life requires a relationship with Him. It may not always be obvious, but His plan is always there. You must embrace it by seeking relationship with the Almighty.

There are many types of conflict with God. One type is the world's continual conflict with God by refusing His existence and His offer of relationship. If you choose not to become a Christian, the natural state of your life will be at conflict with God. He is not at conflict with you, but you are with Him by your own freewill and avoidance of His blessings.

Another type of conflict is where you believe in Christ as your Savior but do not develop your relationship with Him to the fullest. You may love God but do not understand His Word or the gifts that He has for your life. Not understanding your relationship with God can put you in conflict with Him. Conflict between friends is avoided the more time you spend understanding each other.

> *"Because the carnal mind is enmity against God: for it is not subject to the law of God, neither indeed can be."*
>
> *(Romans 8:7)*

The natural, or carnal, world and the thoughts of men are in opposition to God's way of thinking. The mind of God does not operate the way our physical brain does. He thinks in terms of holiness and righteousness. No evil thought can be entertained in His presence. *"For My thoughts are not your thoughts, nor are your ways My ways," says the Lord. "For as the heavens are higher than the earth, So are My ways higher than your ways, and My thoughts than your thoughts." (Isaiah 55:8-9 NKJV)*

God is often blamed for all problems.

Have you ever watched the news? My daughter likes to tell the joke that the evening news starts out with a hearty "Good Evening" by the newscaster as he proceeds to tell you all the reasons it isn't. The news ranges from scandal, death, bad weather, disaster, crime, and sports. It seems strange, but sports are often the most redeeming part of the news.

It is the only "impartial" section where just the facts are mentioned. Much of the "bad news" is blamed on God through the mouth of the newscasters or people they interview.

It is easy to see why many people have trouble following God if He is blamed for all the problems in the world and in their life. I remember watching a newscast some years ago where people were caught in a flash flood that swept away their house and all their belongings. Fortunately, the people were rescued by helicopter. When interviewed, the quote went something like this, "Why did God destroy our house? What have we ever done to deserve this? It is not fair!"

Now that is a pretty tough blame to cast on God. Later the news mentioned the home was built in a flood zone that was prone to such incidents. Now, whether or not the people knew this, our hearts should go out to them in their time of distress. But God should not be blamed for the man's oversight of building areas. All too often in life we blame God for all the things that do not go according to our personal plan. We should not spend time thinking about what God is doing to us. Instead, we should take the higher thought and think about what God can do through us.

Another example of conflict with God is simply denying the call God has for your life. I know from experience that we can run from God all of our life, but I have some advice for everyone; God runs faster. It's that Omni-present talent of his.

The prophet Jonah spent much of his energy trying to evade God's desire for him to preach salvation to the Ninevites. Jonah despised the Ninevites and did not want to go near their city. In his attempt to escape God's plan, Jonah sailed to a far away land only to be thrown overboard by a superstitious crew and was then swallowed by an enormous fish. *"Now the Lord had prepared a great fish to swallow Jonah. And Jonah was in the belly of the fish three days and three nights." (Jonah 1:17 NKJV)*

"God don't make no junk."

Jonah spent three days inside a putrid fish before he realized he couldn't get away from God and agreed to preach in Nineveh. Although still not desiring to go, God delivered Jonah to Nineveh. Jonah preached the message God gave to him. The people repented and the entire city was saved. *"So the people of Nineveh believed God."* *(Jonah 3:5 NKJV)* Our obedience to God brings blessing to us and others.

Every single person on the earth has gifts bestowed on us by God. It is up to us to find that gift and open it for the good of all humanity. We are each created unique by the Creator himself. As my kids used to say, "God don't make no junk." Often, we need to remind ourselves of God's love and that we are His children. Life's circumstances often cloud our view of God.

Circumstances

In 2004 we purchased a house in northern New Jersey. At the time we were enjoying a successful ministry helping our local church and I was enjoying a prosperous position as a financial director in New York City. The house was affordable for my salary and promised to be a great investment as year over year home values in our town increased.

After only two years in the house, our entire life situation changed. My job transferred, we put our New Jersey house on the market, and we moved to Fort Collins, Colorado. We expected a rapid sale of the house which was standard at the time.

Like many others who were caught up in the housing crisis that began in 2006, that was not exactly the way it turned out. Time marched on and the house was still for sale. More time progressed and the house didn't sell. Many price reductions later; the house still had a "for sale" sign in front of it. After much anger, frustration, crying and kicking; the house was still for sale. I had no patience and because of it, God's perfect work was delayed.

> *"But let **patience** have its **perfect** work, that you may be **perfect** and complete, lacking nothing."*
> *(James 1:4 NKJV – My emphasis added)*

As time progresses certain things that God is doing become clearer.

My wife and I were both convinced we heard God tell us to purchase the home. I wanted to keep lowering the price and she wanted to hold our price. I was angry with her and at conflict with God for not coming to our defense and salvation more timely. Gretchen and I would argue about the sale price of the house and I would take it out on God. I learned that God is not easily offended. I would really let him have it by venting all of my frustration and anger at Him. I blamed Him for moving us from the security and comfort of Texas. I felt he should honor the fact that we obeyed Him. Thank goodness His thoughts are higher than ours. If God changed His mind or operated on emotion like us we would all be in trouble.

I had a difficult time dealing with why it took so long for our situation to become clear. It really was a struggle to have patience. Repeatedly I released the sale of the house to the Lord and His timing. Then I would make a payment along with the hefty property taxes levied in New Jersey and have a nice little fit. "Why do I have to pay these taxes? We don't even live there anymore. God, why are You taking so long!??!?!" After more frustrating conversation with God, (from my end) I would take the situation away from Him and try to fix it myself.

I would check all market conditions and comparable houses and make a significant price drop. Guess what happened? Absolutely nothing happened. I made several of these price drops and all had the same result; nothing. I was so frustrated I even prayed for the house to be hit by a meteor and explode. (How many know that prayer was not likely to be answered…) I even thought of raising the price or even giving the house back to the bank. I nearly lost my faith to believe anything during this process on more than one occasion.

Unfortunately, when you give back a debt you have incurred, you cause someone else to pay for it. Others pay for it through higher fees, higher taxes, or higher national debt. When the government spends money the taxpayers foot the bill. Sometimes it is unavoidable to walk away from a debt. Other times alternatives do exist if we just listen and have some patience.

God calls us to walk and talk with him through every circumstance.

Through the grace of God we managed to make all of our payments and eventually sold the house. At first we had a hard time seeing any blessing in the situation. Since that time we are with both sides of the family in Arizona which is a prayer answered. I am self-employed and able to spend much more time with family compared to the minimal vacation and free time I experienced with corporate America. Being self-employed enabled me to schedule time to write this book.

Certainly, the couple that bought the house enjoyed buying it at such a reduced price and we were able to buy a house in Arizona for less as well. I do know that even though my flesh was constantly "flaring up" we gained a greater reliance on God in the situation. Our commitment to pray for our finances increased and opened windows for God to intervene on our behalf.

So why was the home not selling when we needed it to? In Colorado and later in Arizona, my salary was significantly less than it was New York. The house was threatening to ruin us financially. Eventually, after 20 long months the house sold at a loss and life went on. We wanted the house to sell in our timeframe. God had a different plan. We did not understand it at the time and do not fully understand it all today. As time progresses certain things that God is doing become clearer.

If the house had sold quickly, we would have very likely purchased a home in Northern Colorado. Colorado turned out to be a temporary stopping point on our way back to Arizona. If we had purchased property, we would have slowed down the plan of God to bring us back to our home state. If we were not in transition back to Arizona, my wife may have missed the opportunity to lead her father to the Lord shortly before his death. If we had purchased a home in Colorado, there is no doubt we would be wondering why we were so cold. (We did one winter there. That is enough for a lifetime.)

Walk with God for your sake.

God calls us to walk and talk with him through every circumstance and experience we have. He calls us continually to walk closer with Him, His wisdom, and His ways. Finding the call of God on your life is not a deep seated spiritual understanding that takes ten years of Bible school. It is not found by begging or pleading with God in prayer. It is not found by holding an official position in a church or other religious organization. It is a simple manner of fulfilling two simple rules of life.

> *Rule Number One:* *"You shall love the Lord your God with all your heart, with all your soul, and with all your mind."*
> *(Matthew 22:37 NKJV)*

> *Rule Number Two:* *"You shall love your neighbor as yourself."*
> *(Matthew 22:39 NKJV)*

Operating in Rule Number One is as simple as reading the Bible, attending a Christ-centered church, and talking to the Lord in prayer. It is about a relationship with God. If you do any one of these or all three, God will show up and talk to you. All He requires is that you listen in return. God talks to us through the Bible by thoughts and stirrings in our spirit, through other people, through circumstance, through our spiritual leaders, and in many more ways.

Operating in Rule Number Two creates a selfless attitude because no one hates himself. We clothe ourselves, feed ourselves, watch out for ourselves, and generally take pretty good care of self. We simply need to take the focus off us and treat others the same way. When we consider others more highly than ourselves we find out where our heart is. Where Your heart is shown by where you spend time. "*For where your treasure is, there your heart will be also." (Luke 12:34 NKJV)* Where do you spend your time? Where would you like to spend your time?

Many of us are out of balance with God because we are busy doing our own thing or telling Him what to do. We do not spend time listening when He is trying to tell us something to say or do. The majority of all society claims belief in God. Perhaps they say that claim with hope it will provide good fire insurance. Fire insurance is hope that doing good deeds and good actions is enough to avoid spending eternity in a very hot and bad place.

But a claim of belief is not enough. It is one thing to say something but quite another to live it. Actions speak far louder than words. Jesus said that the world will know his disciples by their fruit, or actions and blessings. *"You shall know them by their fruit." (Matthew 7:20)*

The first part of coming into balance with God is to become a Christian.

Fruit is the outcome of an obedient and submitted life to the will and direction of God. Think of a fruit tree. When first planted, it does not bear large, delicious, healthy fruit. It starts out as a seed, then a small sprout, a sapling, and after careful cultivation it grows into a healthy tree. Over time the tree strengthens and, if still properly cared for, starts to bear fruit. Fruit comes in many forms of blessing such as financial prosperity, physical health, abundant joy, the desire to serve, wish to help other people in need, peace, and confidence.

"Be still and know that I am God."

(Psalms 46:10)

Our lives are so noisy that many times when God whispers to us we fail to hear what He is saying. I used to coach my girls at the local YMCA. At the same time, I was taking them to drama practice, church events, and homeschool activities. My wife and I were also volunteering multiple times a week at several ministries. All these things I was doing were good things. But I was so busy and tired from the effort, my prayer life and Bible reading slowed to a standstill. It seemed I couldn't hear the Holy Spirit talking to me. I know I certainly wasn't talking to Him. I had to eliminate a few obligations to get back on track.

When we are so busy we do not hear our spirit stirring from deep within us. Without God's daily direction, pressures compound on top of each other. The stress and strife of trying to get ahead without God can be disappointing and discouraging. The business of the world alone will keep you away from God's plan for your life and balance.

The first and most important part of coming into balance with God's will for our life is to become a Christian. *"For God so loved the world that He gave His only begotten Son, that whoever believes in Him should not perish but have everlasting life." (John 3:16 NKJV)* How can we be part of the God's overcoming solution when we spend most of our time dealing with this problem laden world?

Submitting our lives to Christ is the single most important action to balance our life. Recognizing you cannot do it all in your own strength but only with Jesus as our Savior is the most important decision you need to make.

If you have not done so, ask Jesus to come live in your heart and make you a new person. Believe He died on the cross for your sins and that you are forgiven. It is that simple. All of your past sin is forgiven and your new life begins immediately. With acceptance of Christ, all of heaven's blessings become available to you. You now work with God instead of against Him.

Who God is and who God says we are.

The second piece of the balance equation is to actually learn more about God. Learning more about God empowers you for breakthrough. Many people take the first step of asking God to forgive them but stop there. It is critically important to learn and study what God says about you. The Bible is the one stop shop for learning who God says He is and who God says you are. It shows examples of God's blessings, His abundance, life lessons, what to say, how to think, how to pray, and how to prioritize the things in life.

Make God your priority, your only priority. If you do, unbalanced things in your life will start to fall into place. He will show you how to heal, recover, and gain momentum away from past mistakes. Better still, He teaches you to learn from past choices and not repeat them. With Jesus as your King, the volume and static of the world is tuned out against His life changing power.

God is not the "big, scary guy in the sky".

While on the learning trail about God, amazing things start to occur. The more time you spend with Him, the more you begin to think and act like Him. Circumstances grow smaller in significance as your heart and mind are focused on God and His love for you. Certain things causing anxiety no longer seem important and fresh, new ideas emerge. Your decision-making becomes more confident and peace begins to invade your life. Where peace is, strife must leave. When you start to think like God as a new creation in Christ; His thoughts begin to be heard above all else.

> *"Therefore if any man be in Christ, he is a new creature: old things are passed away; behold all things are become new."*
> *(2 Corinthians 5:17)*

When you hear God's direction, doorways and pathways begin to open. Your only requirement is to put one step in front of another. The burden to accomplish the work is on God. All you have to do is be a willing participant. He is just waiting for you to step out in faith and follow Him much like He required of the original twelve disciples. If you follow Him, He will direct your path.

God is incapable of failing.

God is not the "big, scary guy in the sky" that perhaps you believed at some point in your life. He is not lording above us just waiting for our next mistake so He can crush us down in defeat. If that was the case, we would all be crushed daily. God does not put failure on us nor does He wish it for us. God is incapable of failing. He cannot be defeated. God is always the truth in every instance, situation, and circumstance. He is not to blame for all of your trouble and disappointment in life. God does not mock you, blame you, or ridicule you for your mistakes.

In fact, God's personality is quite the opposite. What exactly do I mean by that? What is God's personality? Jesus taught, *"If you really know Me, you will know My Father as well. From now on, you do know Him and have seen Him." (John 14.7 TNIV).* He did what the Father did. We need to ask ourselves, "What did Jesus do?" He did the same thing over and over again. Jesus went through all the land teaching, preaching, and healing all who were oppressed of the devil.

> *"And Jesus went about all the cities and villages, teaching in their synagogues, and preaching the gospel of the kingdom, and healing every sickness and every disease among the people."*
>
> *(Matthew 9:35)*

You are a friend of God.

Jesus went about doing good and helping everyone He met. The only people that had issue with Him and His teaching were dishonest and disingenuous leaders who had much to lose if the common people were to have a change of heart. All others, Jesus called a friend. You and I are friends of God. To simplify it further, this describes the entire Bible and Gospel of Christ. Gospel means "good news" and friendship with God is all that really matters to Him. God is your friend and He wants you to know Him better. God requires your time and attention. He is ready to give you His time and attention. All He requires is your time and attention.

> *"And the scripture was fulfilled which saith, Abraham believed God, and it was imputed unto him for righteousness: and he was called the Friend of God."*
>
> *(James 2:23)*

God desires a breakthrough relationship with you. He wants you to hear His voice. God desires you to submit to His direction because you love Him. In your relationship with God, He enjoys when you praise and worship Him in love. When we make mistakes God expects you to repent and know that you are forgiven. Out of love and respect you gain a desire to spend time alone with Him in prayer and Bible study. The fruit of the Spirit is what comes from your breakthrough with God.

> *"The fruit of the Spirit is love, joy, peace, longsuffering, gentleness, goodness, faith, meekness, temperance."*
> *(Galatians 5:22-23)*

Breakthrough with God is an enjoyable friendship with Him. You trust God and God trusts you. You obey God and His Word comes to pass in your life. Obedience to God brings His blessings and breakthrough.

As you spend time with Him you begin to walk and talk like Him. His Spirit begins to permeate every fiber of your being. The blessed and abundant life is what awaits you living your life with God.

GOD

"I am Alpha and Omega, the beginning and the ending, says the Lord, which is, and which was, and which is to come."
(Revelation 1:8 KJV)

Chapter 9 Reflection:

1. Do I have any conflicts with God?

_____

_____

_____

2. Have I given God the priority he deserves in order to achieve balance in my life? Explain.

_____

_____

_____

3. If I have not given God priority, what changes do I need to make to do so?

_____

_____

_____

4. How does God view me?

_____

_____

_____

Prayer to repeat loud:

"Thank you God for showing me how to walk and talk with You. Thank You for delivering me from a life of conflict into a life of peace. Thank You for saving me and guiding me to a breakthrough life. In Jesus name, Amen."

CHAPTER 10

PEACE

"You will keep him in perfect peace, Whose mind is stayed on You, Because he trusts in You".

(Isaiah 26:3 NKJV)

PEACE is a word utilized across the globe on a regular basis. The world is full of people, governments, and programs that promise peace in one way or another. Truly, without God there can be no peace. All of the world's problems cannot be solved with philosophies, medicines, legalities, programs, treaties, sanctions, or monies. Peace can only come from the Creator himself. God's peace brings breakthrough. *"And the **God of peace** will crush Satan under your feet." (Romans 16:30 NKJV-my emphasis added)* True peace is not about world peace on a global scale but the peace that resides within individuals. If mankind accepted God's peace that lives on the inside of us when we accept Christ, world peace would be the outside result.

Man was not meant to "go it alone" in the world. In the beginning, God was with Adam and Eve in the garden walking and talking with them as friends. There was no fear, no conflict, no doubt, and no compromise. There was only safety and peace. Knowing that you are safe in the arms of the mighty Creator and Savior brings about so much peace that life's strongest storms cannot avail against you. God's peace is an inner peace powered by the Holy Spirit. It is a knowing from deep within that you are loved and taken care of.

Peace I leave with you, my peace I give unto you: not as the world giveth, give I unto you. Let not your heart be troubled, neither let it be afraid."

(John 14:27)

"If God be for us, who can be against us?"

(Romans 8:31)

People often relate peace to the natural world that we live in as an almost tangible state of friendliness between individuals or nations. In a conflict or war between countries, there is never peace before war breaks out as there is typically a build-up of tension and hostility. There are reasons for the disagreement which seem valid and strong enough for both countries to enter into a battle. Peace talks may enter into negotiations or conversations, but unless both sides are in agreement, balance cannot be achieved.

Persevere to gain breakthrough.

With no treaty, conflict begins on the battlefield. Fighting is intense, property is destroyed, foundations are rocked, and people's lives are disrupted. Usually, the more prepared, determined, and better equipped side wins. Once the battle is over, something amazing happens. Peace appears on the scene and takes precedence. Accords, treaties, and agreements are signed and people begin to rebuild their lives. It occurs whether or not we are talking about a physical battle or a spiritual battle.

Spiritual Authority

This scenario is what takes place each time we decide to rid ourselves of conflict in our life. Internal and spiritual conflict is as real as a physical battle. God and His angel's war for our victory and the devil and his minions try to keep us in defeat and conflict. *"For this purpose the Son of God was manifested, that He might destroy the works of the devil."* (1 John

3:8) We must battle through conflict to capture our balance. We must persevere to gain our breakthrough.

There can be no God kind of peace inside each of us without understanding our spiritual authority. *"Verily, verily, I say unto you, He that believeth on me, the works that I do shall he do also; and greater works than these shall he do; because I go unto my Father." (John 14:12)* When Jesus walked in earthly flesh, He took dominion over the demons and agents of evil that He experienced. He cast them out of oppressed people and commanded them to leave and not return. *"Where the Sprit of the Lord is, there is liberty." (2 Corinthians 3:17)* Liberty equals freedom and peace.

Christ won every battle due to His preparation in prayer and His uncompromising relationship with the Father. He stood on the side of righteousness and He knew it. Jesus walked in authority and the demons had no choice but to obey. If Jesus did not take His God-given authority over the spiritual realm, His ministry on earth would have been constantly overcome by attacks of evil. These attacks would have distracted, diminished, and potentially consumed the work of God on the earth. Jesus had the authority, but if He did not understand or use it; there would have been no peace, no miracles, no ministry, no cross, no resurrection, and no victory over Satan's conflict.

> *"And Jesus came and spake unto them, saying, all power is given unto Me in heaven and in earth."*
>
> *(Matthew 28:18)*

Through Christ's redemptive work, we have the same authority Jesus had for taking dominion over the spiritually dark elements of this world. We have it because He gave it to us. Through His power and authority we walk as joint heirs together by the grace of God. *"The Spirit Himself bears witness with our spirit that we are children of God, and if children, then heirs—heirs of God and joint heirs with Christ." (Romans 8:16-17)* God has given all believers in Christ the authority to bring balance to the spiritual world around us.

Jesus gave dominion over the spiritually dark elements of this world.

Many of us walk around and do not understand our God-given authority. God entrusts the spiritual well-being of our world to the believer in Christ. Jesus even reminded humanity of this fact as He ascended to the Father. "*Most assuredly, I say to you, he who believes in Me, the works that I do he will do also; and greater works than these he will do, because I go to My Father.*" *(John 14:12 NKJV)* I know for many years I did not understand or even know I had spiritual authority. I went through my daily life and just accepted many of the things that happened to me. When I learned about God's authority it changed my life. God provides us the means, ability, and power to overcome the enemy. "*If the Son therefore make you free, ye shall be free indeed.*" *(John 8:36)*

It is true that God sent the Holy Spirit to be our guide and teacher but He has another purpose. He provides us the power to overcome the adversary. The Apostle Paul taught in the book of 1 Thessalonians 1:4 *(NKJV)* that the "*Gospel did not come to you in word only, but also in power, and in the Holy Spirit and in much assurance.*" The Holy Spirit provides power to us and through us to change the natural and super-natural realm around us. Jesus further empowered us when He said in Mark 11:23-24 that if we speak to any circumstance in faith and do not doubt, God will accomplish it. How does God accomplish His work and power on the earth? He accomplishes it by the power of the Holy Spirit. As a believer in Christ, the Holy Spirit stands ready to assist and empower you in everything.

The Christian sets the spiritual tone for every situation.

We must exercise our ability to combat the forces at work against us. To win our personal battles, we must be prepared. Better still, thanks to Christ we cannot lose. We battle a defeated foe that cannot withstand

Christ's power. We are joint heirs with Christ and because of this we can exercise His authority over both the physical and spiritual realms.

> *"And if children, then heirs; heirs of God, and joint-heirs with Christ; if so be that we suffer with Him, that we may be also glorified together."*
>
> *(Romans 8:17)*

The Christian sets the spiritual tone for every situation he is in if he chooses to do so. A prepared Christian not only brings balance by their faith but pushes back the work of the enemy. When the enemy is slowed breakthrough can occur. Wherever you go and whatever you do can be influenced and changed by working together with God. Every meeting, every location, every situation can be brought into the obedience of Christ by taking dominion over every ungodly thing that interferes with His work. We must speak the Bible, pray the Bible, and do what it says. God responds to His own words. We must act like Jesus did. We do not have to be bystanders and victims of circumstance.

An "executive" decision

Years ago I attended weekly manager meeting with other executives. One particular executive would verbally abuse others in the room to intimidate and force his opinion on everyone to push his view of company direction. He would be especially vicious if anyone was unprepared or responded with like aggression. I did not think much of it at first as everyone seemed to just deal with it as business as normal, although it made me uncomfortable. I did not try to rock the boat and status quo remained until I was the victim of one of the weekly attacks. I was unprepared how to respond. So I basically argued my way out of the situation with facts I had prepared. However, there was no need to experience the harshness of the verbal attack. It was unprofessional and uncalled for. The entire incident really bothered me and I could not let it go.

Darkness cannot withstand the Light.

On the way home I realized that while the "attack" seemed to be happening in the here and now it really wasn't. It was entirely spiritual. That is why I felt so uncomfortable after the incident. The negative forces that were at work in this individual were tormenting everyone in the room and at that earlier moment went after me. I took the issue to the Lord in prayer and learned a valuable truth. No force of darkness can withstand an ounce of light. In fact, darkness flees the light and cannot have fellowship with it. Peace cannot come without action to push back the darkness.

> *"For we wrestle not against flesh and blood, but against principalities, against powers, against the rulers of the darkness of this world, against spiritual wickedness in high places."*
>
> *(Ephesians 6:12)*

I decided I was not going through that situation again and that no one else should have to either. I had forgotten my strongest ally and the one to whom this executive had no authority. Yes, I worked for a company but my true employer was the Alpha and Omega, Prince of Peace, Mighty God, and the Everlasting Father. He was more than willing to assist me in my time of need.

I was prepared not only in the natural but in the spiritual.

With God's help, I purposed to "take" the spiritual authority over the next meeting for the upcoming week. *"Whatever you bind on earth will be bound in heaven, and whatever you loose on earth will be loosed in heaven." (Matthew 18:18 NKJV)* I prayed against the forces of darkness in this person, in the room, and around the entire meeting. As a great pastoral friend of mine in Texas says, "I don't care if it's in him, on him, or around him. Whatever it is cannot withstand the blood of Jesus and the power of the Holy Spirit!" I prayed everyday and especially on the day of the meeting. I felt spiritually supercharged from the outset because through prayer I knew the Holy Spirit had already set the tone in the room before the meeting even started. I was prepared not only in the natural but in the spiritual. I knew the balance of power had tipped away from whatever demonic influence was at work and was now leaning toward righteousness and peace.

The meeting started peaceful enough until something disagreeable to this person was stated by another manager. I started to notice all the anger, frustration, and wickedness come up in this person and he stood up. Before he could boil over I stood up and peacefully, yet authoritatively stated that we were not going to interrupt in the meeting today. No one was going to get upset. I said it with authority and respect. I was careful not to be rude or self-promoting in any way.

With a surprised look on his face, the person sat back down and said nothing. Now that was a miracle all by itself. The meeting continued without one interruption and nobody was verbally ridiculed. The rest of our meetings in the future were similar. They were much more productive and accomplished much. Over time, this person actually became a participant instead of an adversary. Peace ruled and reigned in the room. A breakthrough of peace cannot exist unless we insist that it does.

"Blessed are the peacemakers: for they shall be called the children of God."

(Matthew 5:9)

Think about situations in your life where conflict, not peace, ruled. Why did that happen? I know in my life where I have not chosen to be a peacemaker in a difficult situation, problems only become worse. Either I added fuel to the fire with my attitude, completely ignored the situation, or refused to proactively understand the reasons behind the situation. In any case, the issue was always more extreme and lasted longer. Rationally, it makes no sense to continue in a difficult situation where everyone has the ability to choose to do the right thing. There is real power in taking the authority of peace. Such power allows you to speak in love with authority. Knowing you have peace gives you power and authority. Peace always repels conflict just as light always repels the darkness. The authority and gentle power of peace is ours for the taking if we choose to do so.

Jesus is called the Prince of Peace and the Lamb of God. Yet He is also called King, Conqueror, and Lion of Judah. They are not separate titles; they are unified. Peace with power exists for those who submit their own will to the will of God. Peacemakers give up their right to be right but amazingly end up winning every battle because Jesus wins in peace. Remember, everything in some capacity is a spiritual battle. Your Leader has already defeated spirits, death, hell and the grave.

Walk in the authority of peace.

Have you ever met someone that is always kind and confident? Nothing seems to bother them and they are always helpful. These people walk in their authority of peace. They understand how to cooperate with God to take dominion over the enemies of peace. I watch people like this to learn from them. I strive to gain their wisdom and then utilize what I learn.

The authority of peace is an impenetrable barrier. Spiritual authority eliminates Satan's plans to hurt and destroy. The gospel of peace is a force that cannot be withstood.

> *"Therefore take up the whole armor of God, that you may be able to withstand in the evil day, and having done all, to stand. Stand therefore, having girded your waist with truth, having put on the breastplate of righteousness, and having shod your feet with the preparation of the **gospel of peace**; above all, taking the shield of faith with which you will be able to quench all the fiery darts of the wicked one. And take the helmet of salvation, and the sword of the Spirit, which is the word of God; praying always **with all prayer** and supplication in the Spirit, being watchful to this end with all perseverance and supplication for all the saints"*
> *(Ephesians 6:13-18- my emphasis added)*

Choose the breakthrough of peace instead conflict.

When we walk in peace we have control over what happens to us. Jesus exemplified control through peace when He was put on trial by religious leaders and Pontius Pilate. He was accused, hit, spit on, and ridiculed yet He refused to verbally defend himself. He knew what He was doing and He was in control. Jesus would have actually had to come off of His authority throne to respond to false accusations.

Pilate marveled at Jesus' self control and attitude of calm in *John 19:11-12 NKJV.* He said, *"Don't you know I have the power of life and death over you?"* Jesus calmly answered in reply, *"You have no power over Me but what my Father chooses to give you."* Now that is spiritual authority! Jesus had absolute authority over His situation. No one could take His life; he willingly laid it down for humanity. *"I lay down my life that I may take it again. No one takes it from Me, but I lay it down of Myself. I have power to lay it down, and I have power to take it again. This command I have received from My Father." (John 10:17-18 NKJV)*

At a word, legions of angels would have flocked to Jesus' rescue and destroyed His accusers. *(Matthew 26:53 NKJV)* But *"God so loved the world, that He gave His only begotten Son so we may have eternal life." (John 3:16)* Jesus knew the power He possessed and knew the power of His confession, or words. Jesus did not raise a spiritual army to defend Him. He simply operated in His authority of peace.

Like Jesus, we must choose peace. Peace creates authority. The greatest strength you can have is the confidence of having Jesus' inner peace guiding you through life and its circumstances. Choose to create peace wherever you go. God's peace will change the world. God's peace will change your life. God's peace will change your marriage too. Are you ready?

PEACE

"You will keep him in perfect peace, Whose mind is stayed on You, Because he trusts in You".

(Isaiah 26:3 NKJV)

Chapter 10 Reflection:

1. When Am I a peacemaker?

   _____

   _____

   _____

2. Give an example of when I chose peace instead of conflict?

   _____

   _____

   _____

3. How can I choose to cooperate with God to take my Christian authority?

   _____

   _____

   _____

4. What situations in my life can be changed by submitting them to God?

   _____

   _____

Prayer to repeat out loud:

"Lord, help me to choose peace instead of conflict. I rebuke conflict and strife away from my family, friends, household, and work. Thank You for revealing ways I can work with You to help peace rule and reign in my house. In Jesus name, Amen."

CHAPTER 11

A HUSBAND HEARS

By David Willard

"The man that finds a wife finds a treasure, and he receives favor from the lord."
(Proverbs 18:22 NLT)

S POUSES are like spices. They can heat up your life, add some flavor, give you some extra kick, or give you a sour taste. Spices, like spouses are meant to enhance but, unfortunately, without the right combination become a failed recipe.

Even if you do not have a spouse, these are important chapters for you. You may have a spouse in the future or you may need to give Godly advice to a close friend about their spouse. These concepts are for all inter-personal relationships.

No matter what your marital status, being ready and educated on the marital partnership is very important. Many marital conflicts arise due to people not being prepared for the relationship and the work needed to make it successful.

I have been married many years, most of them happy. My marriage history went something like this. Boy meets girl. Girl then smiles at boy. Boy passes out. Boy asks girl to marry. Girl says yes. Newlyweds go on honeymoon. Back from honeymoon, reality sets in. Have some fights. Make up. Fight some more. After a few years working on marriage, have a good marriage. After a few more years seriously working on marriage, have a great marriage.

Generally, marital conflict begins as soon as a couple gets married. I know that does not sound high and spiritual but it is true. It was certainly true in my life. Conflict started day one and continued until the relationship was nurtured and cultivated like a fine garden. We wanted a fine garden and so did God. If you are familiar with agriculture, cultivation takes a lot of work. The most successful marriages take daily time, prayer, and consideration. Like a garden, a marriage must be tended daily with gentle hands and gentle words. The word gentle must be partnered with good old-fashioned hard work.

Marriage is meant to "divine" us not to divide us.

We are to join together with one another in marriage and become the ultimate two person team – one man and one woman. Marriage is not a competition or contest with a winner and a loser. If that is your attitude both of you will become losers with a capital "L". A couple must win together. If you do not feel united in your marriage then it is time for a change of heart and a new perspective.

What makes a difference in a marriage?

You can pick up almost any marriage book, secular or Christian, and see the statistics. About half the people that get married get divorced. About half of them get remarried and get divorced again. I don't make that statement with any judgment or condemnation for anyone that has gone through a divorce. God does not operate in condemnation; He only deals with His children in love. *"There is therefore now no condemnation to them which are in Christ Jesus." (Romans 8:1)* Divorces are very difficult and have occurred on both sides of our family. I just want to state the facts for perspective.

The first years of our marriage were not easy. Like everyone, we came to the marriage as two distinct individuals and personalities. We had not learned how to blend our gifts, habits, and traits into a "one-flesh" partnership. *"The two shall become one flesh" (Ephesians 5:31)* No matter how much you love each other, blending two people together is challenging. If you say it isn't, you aren't married.

Today in our marriage we focus everyday to become a better husband and wife, father and mother. Over time the effort is easier as our trust together has become stronger. It wasn't always that way. The first years were very tough and we questioned what we had done. Why had we gotten married? After the honeymoon wears off; if you are not careful real life can rob the joy from your marriage. It happened to us and neither of us was satisfied. Although I didn't know why right away, I was determined to change our marriage for the better. I wanted to have a great marriage; that is the point of being married.

What makes the difference in a marriage?

Gretchen and I sat down and asked each other, "How should we discuss marriage in this book? What is something we have done that has really made a difference in our marriage?" We knew our answers right away.

I learned to listen.

I have always been strong willed with a leadership personality. When Gretchen and I would get in any type of discussion I would always take it personally and get defensive. If you are like me, once you get defensive in a discussion, you never listen. You are only concerned with the next thing you want to say or how to deflect the perceived criticism or blame coming your way.

Part of my defense was to interrupt. I figured that if I could inter-rupt Gretchen from saying things I did not want to hear I could get her to stop. It did work, but Gretchen would only stop out of frustration. Our issues did not go away. They were subdued and came back stronger later. It did not matter if we were discussing work, the kids, the weather, the couch, the car, or our marriage. I always felt I was to blame during any discussion so I would shut it down by interrupting. No doubt I held the title of "The Great Interrupter". It wasn't that Gretchen was verbally attacking me or being rude. I had a personal filter that just wouldn't let me hear the context of what she was saying.

Pride is a killer of marriages.

The truth is that there are many important things in a relationship that need discussion. I didn't think I was perfect but I also didn't want to acknowledge my shortcomings. What I didn't realize was the cause of my problem was pride.

Pride convinces us that we don't need to change and our issues are not that bad. *Proverbs 16:18* tells us pride brings failure and destruction to our life. While I am certain I didn't want failure in my marriage, my unwillingness to change was an open invitation for trouble.

After one heated discussion with Gretchen, I had an incredible revelation. We were always discussing the same issues over and over. My take on the situation was that we had already discussed the problem and there was no need to discuss it again. (Being stubborn is pride). My revelation was that if we were discussing it again, perhaps we hadn't fixed the issue.

Interrupting comes with a really bad side-effect of not listening. After my realization that we continued to discuss the same issues over and over again I started to look inside myself. As a man, I am supposed to take my wife's concerns and help alleviate them. Instead, I was making them worse. I then began to think about why things never changed. It was obvious at this point where my problem was. It was with me.

Share one another's burdens.

Instead of listening and trying to understand what she was feeling, I started to feel responsible and was busy "not listening" trying to figure out where I went wrong or what I could have done to prevent the circumstance. As a man I have a strong desire to try and fix every circumstance and conquer every obstacle; whether I caused it or not. That is really not what my wife wanted. She just wanted to tell me her concerns in a safe and open discussion. Often, listening is enough. For her, sharing concerns alleviated stress and helped foster spiritual health. *"Bear ye one another's burdens, and so fulfill the law of Christ." (Galatians 6:2)*

It took me years to learn this but I think it has really has sunk in; although I still haven't mastered it. Today, I listen to what Gretchen is saying to understand exactly how she feels. I do not take it personal and do not feel threatened by our conversation. Usually a few minutes of intense "listening" allows me to address her concerns. She feels better and I feel better. Based on what is said, we can make plans together to address any situation. It is during the times I do not listen that conflict is invited in our relationship. The simple act of listening transformed my marriage. Listening brought consideration and kindness in my responses and opened our communication to an entirely new level.

Husbands love your wives...

If you don't like the behavior or attitude of your spouse, ask your-self this question. Who do husbands and wives spend the most time with? That's right, with each other. The person that has the majority of influence over your spouse is you. The Bible is clear that a husband has responsibility to assist a wife into becoming all that she can be. It is a husband's job to lead, nurture, grow, and love their wife to be a success.

Carefully read *Ephesians 5:25-33*. It states, *"Husbands, love your wives as Christ loved the church and gave Himself for her. That he might sanctify and cleanse her with the washing of water by the word, that He might present her to Himself a glorious church, not having spot or wrinkle or any such thing, but that she should be holy and without blemish. So husbands ought to love their own wives as their own bodies; he who loves his wife loves himself. For no one ever hated his own flesh, but nourishes and cherishes it, just as the Lord does the church. For we are members of His body, of His flesh, and His bones. For this reason a man shall leave his father and mother and be joined to his wife, and the two shall become one flesh. This is a great mystery, but I speak concerning Christ and the church. Nevertheless, let each one of you in particular so love his own wife as himself, and let the wife see that she respects her husband.*

I had not done my job of sanctifying and loving my wife as Christ loved the church. Christ went through everything just to restore and redeem His church. No task was too big for Jesus and nothing was going to stand in His way in order to love and save His church. He calls husbands to do the same.

No spots, no wrinkles

Take a closer look at verse 5:27 above, *"not having spot or wrinkle or any such thing, but that she should be holy and without blemish."* When a wife falters or stumbles in life, it is the husband that should carefully pick her up and dust her off. When she has fears or troubles, the husband is required by God to do whatever it takes to make sure that her concerns are met and she feels safe. A wife with no blemish is confident, loyal, caring, loving, nurturing, and most of all happy. Men, read that passage again. It is your job.

As for me, I wasn't meeting this standard and it was time for a change. Just my understanding of the issue brought balance to our situation. I submitted my concerns to the Lord in this prayer: "Lord, teach me how to listen as you listen. Help me listen to not just the words my wife is saying but the meaning behind her words."

It wasn't easy because I had developed bad habits over the years. From that point on I purposed to listen and not interrupt. Many times I desired to start talking and take over in our conversation. At that point I would just repeat back what I had heard to make sure that I understood what was said. Amazing things began to happen. I soon realized that most of our discussions were not about Gretchen blaming me for issues. Our discussions were her concerns about our relationship, the kids, and where God might be taking us as a family. Most of her concerns did not even relate to my actions but were her thoughts on how to be a better wife and mother. She was taking her role very seriously and I hadn't been along side her providing counsel and guidance.

Every spouse is a gift from God.

Part of our growing together in marriage was learning how to relate to each other. As husbands and wives we each have roles in marriage. They are distinct and when we focus on our own responsibilities, the marriage is strengthened.

Every spouse is a gift from God with ideas, thoughts, emotions, and feelings. It is true for both husbands and wives. My wife is an intelligent, caring, Godly woman. She is educated in her faith, studies her Bible, and has a relationship with God. God has gifted her with understanding in areas that I lack and the opposite is true. A wife's emotions are a husband's spiritual barometer. That barometer can tell a husband the current state of the relationship and if action needs to be taken.

God put gifts in women to complete men, not to compete with men. When Gretchen talks about an issue or situation, I need to listen. She also gives me the courtesy to operate in my spiritual gifts such as leadership, speaking, and fatherhood. Only a foolish husband ignores the Godly wisdom that exists in his wife. God created the woman as helpmeet to ensure sound family decision making.

I was amazed how simple behavior changes like these transformed my marriage for the better. We became closer, more intimate, and our friendship deepened. Conflict melted away. Our relationship became more balanced. We started to see the vision God established for our marriage. We were determined to work and achieve it.

As I practiced my new listening skills I begin to participate in Gretchen's interests, hobbies, and listen to her opinions. I was on my own journey with God to fix my marriage at the same time Gretchen embarked on hers.

A HUSBAND HEARS

"a man shall leave his father and mother, and shall be joined
unto his wife, and they two shall be one flesh."
                                                        (Ephesians 5:31)

Chapter 11 Reflection:

1. What conflicts am I experiencing with my spouse?

    _____

    _____

    _____

2. What steps can a single person do to become more educated about marriage?

    _____

    _____

    _____

3. What can I do to bring balance into my marriage? Read Ephesians 5

    _____

    _____

    _____

4. What scripture speaks most to me about my marriage?

_____

_____

_____

5. What is my perfect idea of marriage?

_____

_____

_____

6. Define steps to achieve your perfect idea of marriage.

_____

_____

_____

Prayer to repeat out loud:

"Thank You father God that I am the husband you want me to be. Give me a vision of what Your perfect relationship is regarding my wife. Thank You for Your grace that empowers me to be the spouse I need to be for You and for my mate. Please show me ways, methods, and ideas to enhance my marriage to build my marriage into a testimony to You and an example for others to follow. In Jesus name, Amen."

CHAPTER 12

A WIFE SPEAKS

By Gretchen Willard

**"Let no corrupt communication proceed out of your mouth,
but that which is good to the use of edifying, that it may
minister grace unto the hearers"**
(Ephesians 4:29)

IT was about one toddler, one newborn, and four years into our
marriage when I wondered why. Why did I get married to be
unhappy? Why doesn't my husband listen to me? What happened to
the love in my heart? I was living my life, but not the ideal and perfect
vision I had in my mind.

We all arrive in marriage with ideas on what will make it a success.

When people get married they come to their new relationship with
all their preconceived notions and daydreams about how wonderful it
will be. It certainly is wonderful, but all of our thoughts and visions do
not come with the challenges and difficulties that are the reality of life.
I knew David was the man for me and I knew that we were supposed to
be married. What I didn't count on was my notions of how I thought
our marriage was supposed to be.

When David would go to work I would happily send him off and look forward to spending time with our two young girls. As the day progressed I began to think about all of the things that were wrong with my husband and our marriage. It made me feel lousy and soon began to affect not only the way I was thinking but my feelings toward David and our marriage. Common tasks became unfulfilling as I thought about all the hardships I was enduring. The thoughts of my mind and the meditations of my heart were negative and self-destructive.

My day progressed with a "poor me" mentality. I wondered why David was at lunch with his business partners while I was at home changing diapers. Why did David get to have a lunch-time Bible study when I was just lucky to have showered before noon? I felt I was trapped at home with no way out.

"Why was I saying and doing things I knew were not fruitful?"

By the time David came home I was ready to let him have it. I have often wondered if my bad attitude made him work longer hours to avoid coming home right away. He knew that if he was five minutes late, I would open the conversation with, "You're late, how am I supposed to know when to have dinner ready?" Or I might say, "Why didn't you call? I was worried."

I didn't always verbally attack or criticize him, but I didn't exactly exhibit the love of Jesus either. When you think about negative things during the day do not expect your words to be edifying and loving in the evening. I knew I shouldn't be saying and acting with so much conflict but I couldn't stop.

It didn't matter if I was on diaper shift or the day shift; in the evening there was always more work like dishes, laundry, and cleaning. My preconceived ideas told me that David should help more when we were home together. Instead of enjoying time after work together it turned into conflict.

I would ask myself, "Why was I saying and doing things I knew were not fruitful?" I didn't want to worry and meditate on the negative things in our life. By all appearances we really had a good marriage. What was going on? I took my situation to the Lord in prayer. "Lord why am I unhappy? There is no reason for it. Please show me what is going on."

The Lord said, "Your thoughts are out of control. Quit thinking so much".

The Lord gave me an answer to my prayer. He showed me that my thought life was out of control and out of the abundance of my heart, my mouth was speaking. The problem was that my heart was not full of God's abundance but negative thoughts, experiences, and emotions I had put in there. My first task was to be quiet. The Lord initially dealt with my actions to immediately remove conflict from my marriage. Then we worked together to change my heart.

He said to be still and know that I am God. *(Psalm 46:10)* Be quiet. That's right; God said to close my mouth. Of course not for all things, but to anything that did not enhance my marriage or glorify Him. Shut off any negative words that were sowing conflict. It was simply the old adage, "If you don't have anything nice to say don't say anything at all." With His help, I purposed to start right away.

The next day when David came home, I didn't ask him any questions. I just greeted him with a hello and a kiss. This went on for weeks and months. I would small talk about things that were of a concern to David, his work, or our family.

Many nights I talked very little and sometimes almost not at all because all of my words were confrontational. Strangely, he didn't even notice what I was doing. I didn't let that slow me down because I was working with the Lord for His glory. As more time progressed changes became more obvious and changes were noticed. The conflict was leaving because I did not start confrontation. Our home was coming into balance but I didn't have my breakthrough. I needed a positive confession but I didn't have one yet.

While I as learning to balance my words, I started seeking what God said about being a wife. I needed a change of heart. I studied the Bible daily and an amazing thing occurred. I began to see myself as God saw me, not as I had always seen myself. The scriptures were teaching me what it meant to be a wife.

One of the passages in the Bible that I began to mediate on regarding a wife in marriage is found in *Ephesians Chapter 5:22-24 and verse 33.* *"Wives, submit to your own husbands, as to the Lord. For the husband is the head of the wife as also Christ is the head of the church; and He is the Savior of the body. Therefore, just as the church is subject to Christ, so let the wives be to their own husbands in everything. Nevertheless, let each one of you in particular so love his own wife as himself, and let the wife see that she respects her husband.*

You will be amazed and what God will do with your willing heart.

I began to meditate on the above passage that is all about trust and respect.

A woman is instructed to submit to her husband just as a couple is to submit to each other and submit to God. *"Wives, submit to your own husbands, as to the Lord." (Ephesians 5:22 NKJV)* Submission is a very powerful tool that God honors above all else. It can melt the heart of a husband to Christ. I know it melted the heart of mine.

God requires we submit our heart to Him in order to become a Christian. Take a look at this verse, *"Submit therefore to God Resist the devil and he will flee from you." (James 4:7 NASB)* The only way the devil will leave us alone is when we submit to God. Likewise, the only way a marriage can be successful is through submission. Submission is a position of power. Submitting brings God's authority, power, and ability into all situations.

I was submitting for God. Not just for myself or for my husband; although we both reaped the benefits. I submitted to David in actions, but the true submission was to God in my heart. I was doing what God wanted me to do. He knew what was best for my marriage.

I want to point out that God never intends us to submit in any situation that results in a sin against Him. Nor does God want us to submit in any situation that commits a crime against any legal authority. Submission is a tool to win the hearts of others to Christ and live in the blessings and victory of God. It is not blind obedience to the wicked hearts of ungodly people.

In my continued search through the Bible I began to meditate on *Proverbs 31.* Meditating on these verses profoundly changed the way I thought about myself and my marriage. Reading Proverbs 31 is a must. Make it a personal prayer for you. *"She will do him good and not evil all the days of her life." (Proverbs 31:12)* Was I being a good wife by attacking him when he came home? I don't think so and the scary alternative was that I must have been doing evil to him and my marriage. I certainly did want to be an evil wife but a kind and gentle one.

I put myself in a position to seize victory out of conflict.

Our marital conflict was melting away before my eyes. God was mending my heart and changing the way I thought about myself, my husband, and my marriage. It did not happen overnight but as I continued to nurture my relationship with God and think about His Word. I put myself in a position to seize victory out of conflict. I submitted my heart totally to God and gave up my right to be right.

Victory in marriage comes when we lay self down and submit to the authority of Christ. Only through our submission to Jesus can we have success with our spouse. Only through working together with Christ can we change our vocabulary and eliminate words of conflict. Harmful words chip away at your marriage foundation and leave it weak.

If we are honest there is always enough blame to go around between our actions or inactions. Where we go, what we do, what we say, how we say it, and how we act are always solely and entirely up to us. In marriage, it is not about the "me" and "I" but about the "we" and the "us". We must consider our spouse more important that we are. *"A new commandment I give unto you, That ye love one another; as I have loved you, that ye also love one another." (John 13:34)*

If you begin to love the "we" and the "us", you are on the road to a great marriage. Give up your right to be right. When you do, your confession will not just turn away from negativity, but will become the nurturing heart of God that heals and transforms your marriage.

When your heart changes, you will understand your position and responsibility in marriage. Husbands have a role. Wives have a role. They also have a role together for family, for ministry, and for others. That role is to have a blessed, happy, and fruitful marriage.

> *"Submitting yourselves one to another in the fear of God."*
> *(Ephesians 5:21)*

My conflict came from not preferring David more highly than myself. He learned to listen without judgment. To this day, these are the two great commandments of our marriage. I have made it a habit meditate on the good and not the bad. But it still takes a daily commitment to God, my marriage, and my husband. Many people know what to do to improve their marriage but are afraid to do it thinking it won't work. Breakthrough does not exist in fear but in trust. Trust God and put trust in your spouse. You will be amazed and what God will do with your willing heart and Godly words.

A WIFE SPEAKS

> **"Let no corrupt communication proceed out of your mouth, but that which is good to the use of edifying, that it may minister grace unto the hearers"**
> **(Ephesians 4:29)**

Chapter 12 Reflection:

1. What conflicts that I experience are a result of my words?

   _____

   _____

   _____

2. What are the top three things I love about my spouse? (meditate on them):

   _____

   _____

   _____

3. What scripture do I need to meditate on to make me a better wife?

   _____

   _____

   _____

4. Am I submitted to the Lord? How?

   _____

   _____

Prayer to repeat out loud:

"Thank You father God for showing me how to speak life and love into my marriage. Give me a submitted heart to Christ so I can share His love with my husband and family. I thank You that I have a breakthrough marriage. In Jesus name, Amen."

CHAPTER 13

WORDS

"Death and life are in the power of the tongue: and they that love it shall eat the fruit thereof."

(Proverbs 18:21)

WORDS are spoken all the time. Every day people say or do things that influence you and you impact other people. These can be positive or negative interactions. Which way it goes depends on you. There are many negative people out there ready to share complaints and vent anger to anyone that will listen. You do not have to accept their conflict into your life.

Your response to conflict is as important as what you hear and who is around you. Be polite and smile without letting the negative force of their words into your soul. You do not have to agree with all the words you hear, but do not neglect the opportunity for ministry. If you ask, God will show you how to befriend or cooperate with challenging people.

Take control over what you see and do with others. You do have the ability and the resourcefulness to have balance with the people around you. The majority of associations in your life are by choice. You control much of your schedule in life. Do not let others take that away from you, not even family.

How do you react to those around you?

How do you react to those who are angry with you or have hurt you? How do you react when you are angry at another individual? If any of your responses to these questions made your situation more difficult then it is time for a change. You control your actions and reactions.

Many of your reactions are the results of choices you have repeated over time. You may not even realize why you react certain ways. Balance comes in when you recognize how your responses affect others. Breakthrough comes when you realize you can improve situations you are involved in by changing the "I" part of your equation.

God has given you spiritual authority over all things that are not in obedience to the will of God. Good always triumphs over evil in the spiritual realm. God always causes us to triumph in Christ Jesus.

"Now thanks be to God who always leads us in triumph in Christ, and through us diffuses the fragrance of His knowledge in every place."

(2 Corinthians 2:14 NKJV)

You can create the breakthrough life with your words.

On a basic level, if you do not open your mouth, no words will be loosed from it. Words are very powerful and creative. Our words speak life or death. The wrong words create conflict with people. The right words bring balance and breakthrough.

Choose to speak life giving words to people. You can create the breakthrough life with your words. The Bible is rich with instruction about our words and mouth. The following scriptures relate to our mouth and how our mouth relates to our life and lives of other people:

"Pleasant words are as honeycomb."

(Proverbs 5:3)

"Blessed are the peacemakers for they shall be called the children of God."

(Matthew 5:9)

"Out of the abundance of the heart the mouth speaks."

(Luke 6:45)

As the above scriptures show, speak life, pleasant words, and peaceful words. Begin to frame the world around you with what you speak. Have you ever spoken something and instantly regretted it? Did it bring conflict? We have all done that at one time or another. On the other hand, have you ever said something that brought comfort to another? Which gets you a better reaction? Every word we speak is a choice. Will it be positive? Will it be negative? Will it hurt? Will it help? Will it destroy? Will it create? Will it curse? Will it heal?

My pastor in Texas always said, "What you are speaking today is where you will be tomorrow, next week, and six months from now." If you are speaking fear and anxiety you will reap them down the road. If you react in anger towards others, you can be sure others will become angry with you.

Words are very powerful. In *Genesis Chapter 1*, God framed the universe by speaking it into existence. Like God, we frame our small universe by speaking. If you speak encouragement into your friends, co-workers, or spouse, encouragement returns. If you speak anger, anger returns. It is really a simple concept. Practicing the concept will bring incredible breakthroughs to your life.

I am a living example of the power of breakthrough words that removed people conflict from my life. As we talked about in the marriage chapters, the first few years of my marriage were challenging as my wife and I walked through how to have a successful marriage. My wife had the opportunity to come to Christ first and she (and Christ) completely changed her vocabulary toward life and toward me. She started to speak encouraging and supportive words toward me even when I was not doing so with her. She also stopped speaking negative words in regard to our marriage and me. Her actions really made me question what I believed (or didn't believe).

I really did not understand that I had to choose God.

I was in a dangerous situation. I believed I was already a Christian because I went to church as a child and a small amount as a teenager. I knew all of the Bible stories and was a "good person". Have you ever met anyone that thought they were automatically in God's Kingdom because they were a "good person"? The "good person" syndrome affects many people within and without the church walls. People really feel that being a good person is enough to recompense a lifetime of not serving and believing God. The reality is that if we do not submit our life to God we claim we are the master, not Him.

That describes my situation exactly. After all, how could God refuse someone like me who tried to be nice and always tried to do the right thing? Of course I was judging myself and we generally have a lot of grace and forgiveness toward our intents. I really did not understand that I had to choose God. He already had chosen me, but I needed to make a purposeful decision to serve and follow Him. The Bible talks about the man being won to Christ by the chaste conversation of his wife in her obedience to Jesus. *(1 Peter 3:1)* That is exactly what happened to me.

After several weeks I realized that my wife was radically different than the person she was before she gave her life to Christ. Although we sometimes fought and did not always treat each other like we knew we should, I certainly loved her immensely. However, before my very eyes she was becoming nicer, sweeter, more intelligent, more loving, and I could not understand it. At first I thought it was some sort of act or trick that was leading up to something like, "Honey, will you buy us a new car?" However, we did not need a new car. What a mystery. I was either going crazy, the body snatchers had arrived, or my wife was becoming the most incredible woman on planet earth. (I admit it, I am totally biased here).

The truth was that knowledge of Jesus had changed her life so immediately and completely that she was literally walking and talking the way Christ encourages us to do. A few more weeks more and I couldn't stand what was happening. Gretchen was so happy and full of life and even though I have always been a positive person, I did not have what she had. I wanted it. I wanted to experience what had happened to her. I realized quickly that I was not the Christian I thought I was. I soon bowed my knee to the Savior.

Her excellent words are what brought me to the amazing grace of the Savior. I had never had someone treat me so important when I knew I had not done anything to deserve it. That is what hit me. That is exactly what Jesus did for us on the cross. He totally and completely gave His life for us so we could be forgiven and spend eternity with Him.

Choose your words carefully and wisely.

The wonder of Christ's love as it is available to all through His Word that is given to us. People can show it to you or you can show it to the people you meet. That is the idea behind the gospel of good news that Jesus preached. Choose your words carefully and wisely. We have no idea of the lives we can change by speaking encouragement into everyone we meet. Speak the things to people that you want to hear. Those words will return back to you. What we say and how we act will return to us in the words and actions from others. Your life will also be blessed when you say words of encouragement and lift up others.

"Whatsoever a man soweth, that shall he also reap."
(Galatians 6:7)

Galatians 6:7 is a promise for all of us that inspire us to speak out things that you want to receive back. Close off words that people speak to you that are not edifying. When someone says something bad to you or about you ask this question, "Does it agree with what God says about me?" Just because someone says something does not make it true.

This even applies when you hear words regarding another person. Are the words in agreement with what God says about them? If not, make sure you do not judge the person or repeat the words. Only operate in the words God says you are and God says others are.

What you say really does matter to others just like what they say to you matters. Remember, the only person you can change is you. Your words will change the environment around you and cause breakthrough in every facet of your life. The breakthroughs will be for you and those around you. Words are that powerful. They impact more than just us.

Together, we are God's people. We are joined together by our common creation, our common destiny with Him, and our ability to speak words of life to one another. God spoke His Words to create life. We must speak words of life to have successful relationships and have a breakthrough marriage.

WORDS

"Death and life are in the power of the tongue: and they that love it shall eat the fruit thereof."

(Proverbs 18:21)

Chapter 13 Reflection:

1. Do my words tear down or edify others around me?

_____

_____

_____

2. What words of encouragement can I speak that I don't today?

_____

_____

_____

3. How can I build a strong foundation for my life based on my words?

_____

_____

_____

4. My words can push relationships into breakthrough. What do I say?

_____

_____

_____

Prayer to repeat out loud:

"Lord, Thank You that I speak words of life. Remove the words in my life that do not edify and encourage my family and others. In Jesus name, Amen."

CHAPTER 14

A MARRIAGE FORGIVES

"A man shall leave his father and mother, and shall be joined unto his wife, and they two shall be one flesh."
(Ephesians 5:31)

A husband and wife should be best friends. I don't want to be away from my spouse more than I must. We enjoy spending time together because we have both purposed to make each other the best we can be. Marriage should be the best thing that ever happened to a man and a woman. It is God's lifelong gift to His children.

"Then the LORD God said, it is not good for the man to be alone. I will make a helper who is just right for him."
(Genesis 2:18 NLT)

God put one man and one woman together in marriage to help each other. It is the marital relationship that completes us in body, soul, and spirit. It is this relationship where we will learn the most about God and ourselves. It is the relationship that will carry us through good times and difficult times. It is the relationship that is a blessing and not a detriment to our lives. Adam could not achieve his full potential without Eve. As a married person, you cannot achieve your full potential without your spouse.

Your walk as a married couple with Jesus is not separate from the marital relationship but very inter-connected. He must be involved in all aspects to bring breakthrough success. You cannot have good children, or a good prayer life, or a good anything for God if you have a bad marriage. If you are not in complete agreement with your spouse your prayers are not as effective as they can be. *"Being heirs together of the grace of life; that your prayers be not hindered."* *(1 Peter 3:7)*

A marriage that succeeds becomes an example for others to follow. Couples that love each other strengthen their family, church, and community. A man and woman in marriage unity have powerful and effective prayers. *"The effectual fervent prayer of a righteous man availeth much."* *(James 5:16)* As my marriage was healed, our prayer life increased. As our prayer life increased so did our blessings, happiness, and our ability to help others.

We also began to understand the importance of the marital relationship God placed in our lives. He takes it very serious and we should too. Marriage is not the casual agreement the world portrays it to be. It is a covenant.

A Covenant

So what exactly is a covenant? A covenant is a formal and binding agreement between two people. It is a sealed contract that is not meant to be broken. When God gave us the word and institution of marriage, He meant it for life and did not want the marriage to be broken. *"So then, they are no longer two but one flesh. Therefore what God has joined together, let not man separate."* *(Matthew 19:6 NKJV)* God created His Old and New covenants to come into relationship and agreement with us. That is why we were created. Covenant is God's breakthrough seal for marriage.

Divorce is ultimate marriage conflict - Covenant is the Breakthrough.

The church (meaning people within the walls) is not paying attention to God's first ministry: the marriage. I am the church. You are the church. We are the church. We are all individuals, single and married. When marriages are weak the church is weak. When relationships suffer the church suffers. When a marriage splits the church splits.

Divorce is the ultimate relationship conflict. Never contemplate divorce. Don't even speak the word. Many people casually toss out words such as divorce against their spouse. To what end? No good will come out of it unless that is your ultimate goal. Words are powerful and stick in the mind of the hearer. Using painful words during an argument builds up resentment and hurt that can re-emerge later.

If you have already experienced divorce, God does not deal in condemnation. All is forgiven and all is made new with Christ. God only deals with his children in love to ensure there is no condemnation or guilt.

A covenant marriage is a breakthrough marriage. It is when two people put all their individual needs and differences aside to blend into one relationship. A covenant marriage puts the other person first after God – no matter what happens. Covenant blends two people and personalities into *"one flesh"* both physically and spiritually.

Why is there trouble in Marriage?

Trouble begins with unforgiveness which leads to anger and resentment. Many people go through life angry at themselves, angry at others, or angry at their spouse. There are many reasons why people choose not to forgive. All of them revolve around hurt or fear of being hurt.

When we have unforgiveness and anger toward another we are simply stating that we are more important than they are. Scripture tells us that if we want forgiveness we must first remove the issues out of our own life before telling others about their issues. All people tend to view others faults as bigger than they are and view their own shortcomings as insignificant. *"You hypocrite, first take the plank out of your own eye, and then you will see clearly to remove the speck from your brother's eye." (Matthew 7:5 NIV)* Think about this scripture in the context of marriage. If one partner is constantly upset with the other but never looks at their faults, conflict will always be present. Unforgiveness will cripple a marriage.

Unforgiveness will lead to years of painful and destructive behavior. I know several couples that had trouble in their early marriage and spent years battling each other about who was right and who was wrong. From the beginning, it really doesn't matter who is right and who is wrong. If an offense takes root in a marriage, the couple is both wrong. The Bible talks about how we must not condemn others actions toward us or loved ones for what they do. God is the judge, not us. *"Do not judge others, and you will not be judged." (Matthew 7:1 NLT)*. If we complain about others, we have judged them and we open ourselves up for judgment.

Imagine if all the time and energy these couples spent with their destructive words, negative energy, and painful arguments had been spent learning more about each other and what God says about their relationship. It would have changed their marriage and enhanced their understanding of God.

If a couple is submitting to one another with Godly preference, selfishness and pride cannot prosper. Selfishness and pride are the tools of unforgiveness and the reason for every marital fight, occurrence of infidelity, and divorce that has occurred. We must choose to forgive others so that God can forgive us. *"But if ye forgive not men their trespasses, neither will your Father forgive your trespasses." (Matthew 6:15)* Unforgiveness in our heart blocks God's love from prospering in our life.

One sided fights do not last.

People who are angry, hurt, upset, or not happy will nearly always tell you what is bothering them. Marriage conflict is very personal and packs much energy. When someone is upset or hurt, it takes effort to listen to understand what is really going on and why there is an issue. Unfortunately, people on the receiving end of this information tend to put their defenses up and do not listen to what is being said.

As the saying goes, it takes two to tango, mambo, or two-step. Arguments and fights can only be called such if both parties involved choose to participate. Have you ever seen a boxing match where one fighter doesn't put up his gloves in defense? Or does not go on the offensive? That fight will not last very long if only one boxer is participating. One sided arguments have no strength or energy to continue. And besides, they are usually funny because the argumentative person becomes exasperated and often will stop if the recipient is not fighting back.

In all marriages, conflict takes participation. You can change the conflict by changing you. I would rather participate in forgiveness than conflict. Conflict is upsetting, drains energy, and brings hurt. The person that chooses to forgive and not fight immediately ends conflict and brings balance. But it takes forgiveness by both to bring breakthrough.

Forgiveness is a choice.

I believe many people choose to stay mad rather than forgive their spouse. Why? When people are hurt or angry they do not feel like forgiving each other. People think it is impossible to forgive when they are hurt or angry because they think forgiveness is a feeling. Hurt people believe that the one that hurt them deserves unforgiveness for what they did.

Forgiveness is a choice, not a feeling. When you choose to forgive your spouse it is not always reciprocated. In other words, you may decide not to participate in a fight but that doesn't mean your spouse will make the same choice. Forgiveness does not mean that you agree with what someone else did either. It is a choice to step beyond the circumstance and understand everyone makes mistakes. It will always be easier for one person to forgive than the other because of offense or past hurts. Choose to step up and be the one that forgives first to get rid of conflict.

Apologies never start with "if".

Forgiveness is not just an apology. It is choosing to love someone unconditionally no matter what they said, what they have done, what they might say, or what they might do. In my early marriage Gretchen and I would get in a fight and I figured I needed to apologize. I would say, "If I hurt you, I'm sorry." "If I upset you, I'm sorry"

What I said was no apology. Apologies never start with the word "if". The word "if" is a disqualifier that says you really don't think you did anything wrong. True forgiveness says something like, "I have hurt you, please forgive me." "I'm not sure what I have done, but let's figure it out together so it doesn't happen again." Try it next time you need to apologize. It will make a difference.

We are instructed in the Bible to constantly forgive one another. *"Then Peter came to him and asked, "Lord, how often should I forgive someone who sins against me? Seven times? No, not seven times," Jesus replied, "but seventy times seven." (Matthew 18:21-22)* Forgiveness is not a one time event but an ongoing condition of the heart. Forgiveness is easier when you see people they way you see yourself. You look at your own motives and judge them good but look at others and judge them by their actions.

When you are continually around certain people such as your spouse, children, or even co-workers, you will have disagreements. If you are easily irritated or agitated with others, it is time to walk in more forgiveness. Things will happen every day that test your patience. If your heart is prepared they will not affect you.

Trust

Forgiveness is freely given from a willing heart. Jesus freely gave himself to the world to give us forgiveness of sin. *"But God showed his great love for us by sending Christ to die for us while we were still sinners." (Romans 5:8 NLT)* It is Christ's love that enables us to give and receive forgiveness. We can freely give it but trust must be earned.

Trust is built over a period of years for a married couple. In certain situations that trust can be broken. Rebuilding trust starts with two parts of forgiveness: forgiving yourself and forgiving your spouse. If you are angry your blame is directed at your spouse. But you cannot have anger in marriage without the marriage partnership experiencing weaknesses. Remember the one sided boxing match? If there is weaknesses in marriage generally all gloves are up. Put down your emotional, physical, and spiritual gloves and invite the Holy Spirit to empower you to walk the forgiveness path to trust together.

God meant for us to learn about Him by sharing our lives with another person. Only with all of our boundaries down can the Holy Spirit start to mold and change you into the person God wants you to be. Only with your gloves down can the Holy Spirit transform your marriage into what it can be.

People in successful marriages give up their right to be right. What is gained is a lifetime of joy, happiness, and fulfillment. Marriage hears what each partner is saying. It listens, it grows, and it succeeds together.

A Marriage Forgives

"A man shall leave his father and mother, and shall be joined unto his wife, and they two shall be one flesh."
(Ephesians 5:31)

Chapter 14 Reflection:

1. Is my marriage in conflict, balance, or breakthrough?

    _____

    _____

    _____

2. Name the gifts my spouse brings to the marriage that complete me.

    _____

_____

_____

3. Do I need to forgive myself? For what?

_____

_____

_____

4. Do I need to forgive my spouse? For what?

_____

_____

_____

Prayer to repeat out loud:

*"Thank You father God that I am the spouse You want me to be.
I submit to You and therefore am able to serve and love my spouse
with a God kind of love. Today I choose to walk in forgiveness
toward myself and my spouse. In Christ I am forgiven so I choose to
forgive others. In Jesus name, Amen."*

CHAPTER 15

PARENTING IN LOVE

"There is no fear in love; but perfect love casts out fear, because fear involves torment."

(1 John 4:18 NKJV)

PARENTING children is one of life's most amazing experiences. Seeing them and their wide-eyed view of the world makes you wonder if you ever actually thought like that. I believe the sense of wonderment and excitement with which children see is similar to how God views us. After all you are God's child and as a good parent, He is excited about your life.

One of the biggest events in life is the arrival of children. These little packages of coo and poo bring some of the most powerful feelings you can experience. As they get older the joy and emotions only get larger. (So do the expenses – we have four of them) The Bible speaks often about relating to children. Bookstores have shelves full of how to raise them. Children are a book that is continually written. As parents, adults, and mentors of children, we must be careful to write proper guidance, love, direction, boundaries, and knowledge into children.

Parents are often at a loss.

Parents want their children to obey but are fearful of them making the wrong decisions or getting in the wrong situations as they grow. Conflict always occurs no matter how you relate to children. Why? God gave everyone a free will and children are no exception. Parents are often at a loss about how to raise their kids.

If adults do not pursue their God-given responsibility in the steward-ship of their children conflict awaits. The conflict will either be between the adult and the child or between the child and God as they grow up. It will come in the form of disobedience and rebellion. Conflict with chil-dren is one of the most painful feelings a parent will ever experience.

A conflicted parent/child relationship is painful for everyone close to the relationship. *"Even a child is known by his doings, whether his work be pure, and whether it be right." (Proverbs 20:11)* The Bible states that a child is known by his actions. I submit to you that the adult raising them is also known by the child's actions. What do you think about people that have kids running wild throughout the grocery store? How about when you witness a child throwing a temper tantrum? Likely, both the child and the adult are viewed with some disdain and judgment.

Conflict in children pushes them away from Parents and God.

A child left to their own behavioral whims will bring nothing but conflict to all who know him. The conflict can be with self, parents, siblings, teachers, administrators, and all forms of authority. Conflict with authority will unfortunately push a child further away from God who is the ultimate authority.

I know that when our children do not act right my wife and I feel upset. But we have come to realize that we cannot make all the deci-sions for our children. Children must make their own decisions and if the decisions are bad, there are consequences. These consequences are simply the outcome of their behaviors or actions.

God set up the family to teach children their limitations and bound-aries. It is not the world's job. Family doesn't just mean a traditional dad, mom, and the two kids. Families are made up by birth, adoption, marriage, step-children, foster kids, church family, and people full of

God's love. The family was set up as God's safe environment from which to teach and instruct.

Choice and chores

For example, sometimes one of our children chooses not to eat dinner because it was not what they wanted. That's fine, but there is an outcome for their choice. In life it is important to learn that you do not always get what you want. Especially if what you want is based on selfish motivations. The result is they get the uneaten meal for breakfast the next morning. Our job as parents and adults is to guide and steer them on the right path with the assistance of the Holy Spirit. The right path is toward a relationship with God the Father through the love of Jesus. With children, that path is paved with learning how to make good decisions.

Friday's are usually family movie night at our house. When my oldest son was nine years old my wife and I were out running errands and shopping most of the day. Each child had a very reasonable list of chores and schoolwork to accomplish while we were out. Everyone but my oldest son easily completed their tasks and was playing when we returned. I was upset for my son that he chose not to work that day. As a parent I always want my children to behave and I also want to make my children happy. The balance can be a struggle in the flesh.

My best intentions do not build character if I allow my children to shirk their responsibility. The consequence was early bed time and no movie night for our son. Why did I send him to bed? Out of his mouth came these words, "I was too tired to work and do school." It made perfect sense to send him to bed.

It is not an easy decision to remove privileges from your children and I worried that he would be upset and miss the lesson in all of it. Amazingly, he woke up the next morning and did everything he needed to do before noon. He learned a valuable lesson and so did I. His lesson was responsibility and mine was showing love to my son by giving him an unwanted result for his actions.

You cannot negotiate adult perspective to a young, childlike mind.

Many times I have witnessed a frazzled parent trying to negotiate with a child. I have news for everyone. You cannot negotiate your adult perspective with a young, childlike mind. A child's experience and perspective is nothing like that of an adult. Children must be trained by boundaries, example, and most importantly, consistent love. Training in love is the key to bringing balance and boundaries to the life of a child. God deals with us in love as parents need to with their children.

> *"Train up a child in the way he should go: and when he is old, he will not depart from it."*
>
> *(Proverbs 22:6)*

"No" means "no" to a child. If you say "no" and do not back up a request with some type of loving discipline or privilege removal; you are training your child to believe what you say doesn't matter. Remember, there is no fear in love. *"There is no fear in love; but perfect love casts out fear, because fear involves torment." (1 John 4:18 NKJV)* Do not raise your voice or ever train, discipline, or correct your child if you do not have your peace and cannot act in love. There is no such thing as fear in love.

It is the job of parents to steward children.

It is the job of parents to steward belief and trust in God through adolescence, teen years, and adulthood. We must speak life giving words and blessings into the lives of our young people at every given opportunity. As parents we try to teach our children to obey us because the ultimate goal is to have them learn how to hear and obey God's voice. Conflict can come from an improper focus when parents are more concerned with how their kids make them look than what is going on inside.

As children grow and age, they naturally express more independence as they literally do become more independent. It is quite normal, for every child needs to learn how to function as an adult. They are able to do more and more things without the assistance or supervision of an adult. Yet our children still need guidance.

If children do not have leadership from a responsible adult they will seek it from other means such as friends, boyfriends, girlfriends, peer groups, or even gangs. *"A child left to himself bringeth his mother to shame." (Proverbs 29:15)* Additionally, they will grow distant and aloof toward parents who have given away their authority by not enforcing boundaries, setting consequences for actions, and loving the child no matter what the circumstance.

The heart of a child is in all of us.

For years my wife and I parented our four children focused on love and boundaries with consistent, caring discipline. Since we homeschool, our environment was easily set by us. We did our best to guide and guard our children's heart toward the Lord but something was missing as they got older. We noticed some of the ways we parented was ineffective. We wanted our children to choose the right thing because they *wanted* to, not because they *had* to.

We were result oriented parents. It was our belief that for children to succeed we needed to set attainable goals. We did this in school, with chores, and with activities but they never seemed to enjoy what they were doing. Tasks were not unreasonable, but to the kids they were unfulfilling.

Our results were good but our parental style was all wrong. Although we didn't realize it at the time, we were more concerned about the kid's actions over their heart. We had obedient children but there was a lack of joy in the house and within the hearts of both children and parent. We could take them anywhere and they would behave well. But fear of doing something wrong is what motivated them, not loving obedience from their heart. It seems we too were caught up in ensuring the right behavior without bringing their heart along to the results. We would take their behavioral failures as a lack of parenting skill by us. We parented out of fear of failure as parents. It wasn't working.

Gretchen earnestly began to seek the Lord about where we were missing it. What was the key? Here is what the Holy Spirit began to reveal to us.

Understanding the "why" brings balance to parenting.

We all have choices. Every choice has an outcome or consequence. Our children make choices everyday about what they will do or not do. As parents we must guide them to Godly choices in their life. When a child's choice results in a negative outcome a consequence occurs. The outcome depends on the infraction. A child's heart is stewarded by their realization that poor choices have poor results.

For example, if one of our children chose to not complete schoolwork; the consequence would be a late night of study until it was completed. If one of our children told us a lie; then discipline or removal of a privilege would result. We were no longer burdened by the "what" that was occurring. We stopped being upset by their poor decision making and stopped taking the responsibility of their decision making on us.

Children are responsible for their actions. Knowing this takes the burden of responsibility off of the parents. We taught them right from wrong from the Bible. After they know the truth, it becomes their responsibility to make the right choices. Consequences are always made in love.

We began to steer the hearts of our children toward proper behavior by holding them accountable for *the reason* behind their actions. We started to get to the heart of every issue. It is not the *"what"* a child does but understanding the *"why"* they did it that will enable you to change their heart. Very importantly, fear of failure is removed from parenting and replaced with a spirit of love. Parenting from the negative of fear will not be effective in the long run. Only parenting in love will bring lifelong parental success.

Jesus looks at the intents the heart.

Jesus treated all of His disciples the exact same way. He did not go around trying to control their behavior, giving stern lectures, or insulting their intelligence when they made mistakes. Controlling others is not only impossible it is frustrating. Children are no exception. Jesus just brought forward the "why" certain decisions were made or about to be made. He was not offended when the disciples messed up. In fact His attitude was the opposite. Jesus was upset because He knew that their behavior or attitude would be detrimental to them in the future. He focused on getting them to understand why they did something and take the focus off what they did. Jesus always focused on drawing hearts to Him.

For example, Jesus knew Simon Peter was going to deny him three times. Was Jesus upset? Yes he was, but not for Himself. Jesus was concerned because He knew the guilt, shame, and condemnation that would happen in Peter if he followed through on his denial. The key to the following passage of scripture is not Peter's denial but the focus by Jesus on the *heart* of the issue. Look at what Jesus told Peter in *Luke 22:31-34 NKJV*. *"Simon, Simon! Indeed, Satan has asked for you, that he may sift you as wheat. But I have prayed for you, that your faith should not fail; and when you have returned to Me, strengthen your brethren." But he said to Him, "Lord, I am ready to go with You, both to prison and to death." Then He said, "I tell you, Peter, the rooster shall not crow this day before you will deny three times that you know Me".*

Jesus' focus was on Peter's eternal salvation and victory over Satan; not that he was going to make a mistake. Jesus helped Peter overcome by praying for him to have strength in his coming crisis of belief. We must have the same concern toward children. They will make mistakes but if we focus on the ultimate goal of serving God, love will abound.

"The just man walketh in his integrity: his children are blessed after him."

(Proverbs 20:7)

Adults must always set the example. Children want and need to be led by the loving yet firm hand of a parent. Parents must assume their mantle of leadership within the home. For the past few decades parental authority has dwindled in society due to a lack of character from adult leaders and a lack of training given to children.

Bridges of relationship

It is never too late to reel in a child of any age and bring them back to a closer relationship with both parents and God. However, it is much easier to do so when young and much more difficult the older a child becomes. As they get older techniques must change from simple parental boundaries to building bridges of relationship. The older the child is the longer and sturdier your bridge must be. What do I mean by building bridges of relationship?

Foster relationship with all children.

Bridges of relationship are methods and activities that will help a child regain relationship with a parent. If an independent or wayward child loves to watch movies, an invitation to a quality movie by a parent can be a start. You must find out the interests of your child and foster fellowship and trust by actively pursuing those activities.

Agree on an activity. Set some rules to follow such as what topics need be avoided, and focus on having fun. As the relationship begins to be restored trust will return. The parent or adult in charge of a wayward child has the greater responsibility to repair and restore fellowship. Adults need to swallow their pride in order to reach down and save a child from destruction, self-degradation, and lawlessness. It is the adult who is the anchor in the relationship. Younger, immature people cannot be expected to always make mature decisions.

Flesh can get in the way. Our human flesh of emotions and feelings can cloud our judgment. Many parents get tired of dealing with young people and lack the desire or energy to pour fresh teaching, love, and guidance into their children daily. That is where a balanced life must take over the situation. Where are you spending your time? What is keeping you from building bridges of relationship? If you could start over with your children, what would you do differently?

The Breakthrough is to parent in love and not fear.

It can get worse than not enforcing boundaries and rules. If it is commonplace in the home to try to verbally convince a child to have certain behavior and there is never consequence for disobedience; your child is being taught you are a liar. If you ask a child to do something and they don't, you must follow-up. Otherwise your words become meaningless.

Ironically, that convincing is done by an adult that only wants improved behavior. Parents must "win" every battle with the will of a child, no matter how long it takes. Parenting in love will take time. Let me give you an example.

You can't afford not to spend your time on your children. When our oldest daughter was very young we were preparing to go out to an evening meal. Right as we were leaving she had a small "flesh-fit", removed her shoes, and threw them on the floor. Proverbs tells us that *"foolishness is bound up in the heart of a child." (Proverbs 22:15)* There is no understanding why they do what they do, it is just foolishness. All children do "stuff" that makes no logical sense to an adult.

At that moment, my wife and I had a choice. We could have picked the shoes up and put them back on our daughter. We could have yelled at our child. We could have just put her in the car and worried about the shoes later. We did something else.

We never lost our cool, got upset, our lost peace.

For the next several hours we sat with our daughter on the floor and with loving perseverance and training insisted she pick up her shoes and put them on. Yes, she knew how to put her shoes on. It is extremely important to only insist a child do what they have been taught. Do not expect a child to know how to do something you have not shown them or they have never done.

As our daughter continued to refuse, we continued to make minor corrections to her with a big smile on our face. We never lost our cool, we never got upset, and we never lost our peace. We knew we were in control and our daughter was not. Eventually, she submitted her will to our request and happily put on her shoes. She was testing us and we did not want a failing grade. We may have lost our evening out, but we gained our child's soul from the enemy's ploy of disobedience. It is the enemy that wants to destroy our peace and your child's future. We won in love by outlasting her flesh and waiting until she calmed down. After that she was able to easily put her shoes back on. In doing so, we won her heart and respect.

> *"Correct thy son, and he shall give thee rest; yea, he shall give delight unto thy soul."*
>
> *(Proverbs 29:17)*

A parent's ultimate goal is to raise Godly children.

The ultimate breakthrough is to have your children grow up with love and respect for the Lord. There is no reason why a child should stray from the path of righteousness to dance with the world. Scripture promises that if you raise a child up in the way he should go he will not depart from the protection, blessings, and salvation of the Lord. *(Proverbs 22:6)* Just as the great commission commands believers to go make disciples of men; a parent's great commission is to teach, train, and disciple our children in love.

"As for me and my house, we will serve the LORD."

(Joshua 24:15)

Children naturally trust their parents.

There is immense trust in a child's heart. When my children were young I would set them on the bed and take a few steps away from the bed and tell them to jump. (Note: I only did this with one child at a time.) Do you know what they did? They jumped right off the bed and into my arms. Never once did I let them fall or drop them. They simply trusted me because children find it easy to trust. It is that simple trust we adults must fight to retain and what we must nurture in our children toward God. As dedicated parents we must also trust them because trust and love conquers all.

"Love is patient and kind. Love is not jealous or boastful or proud."

(1 Corinthians 13:4)

When it comes to our children, every minute counts. Every word counts. Everything we do concerning them counts. It all counts for their growth and salvation. You can do it. God would never have called you to parenthood or as an adult authority figure over a child if he did not equip you first. Lean on Him for your confidence. Trust in Him. Believe in Him. He will not let you down.

PARENTING IN LOVE

"Children are a heritage of the LORD."

(Psalm 127:3)

Chapter 15 Reflection:

1. What areas of conflict do I have with my child (children)?

   _____

   _____

   _____

2. Am I considering the needs of my child, or my needs, when I say yes or no?

   _____

   _____

   _____

3. What actions do I need to change to bring balance to my child's life?

   _____

   _____

   _____

4. Have I drawn the heart of my child toward God? How?

   _____

   _____

_____

5. Am I training and teaching my children in love or parenting in fear?

_____

_____

_____

_____

_____

_____

6. Am I willing to build bridges where a relationship has been damaged? What do I need to do?

_____

_____

_____

7. How can I work with God to bring a breakthrough to my child (children) and my family?

_____

_____

_____

Prayer to repeat out loud:

"Lord, thank You that I have the wisdom to train and teach my children in the way they should go so that when they are older they will never depart from You. Thank You that through my example of God's love, they will live a life that represents Your love for all people. In Jesus name, Amen."

CHAPTER 16

STEWARDSHIP

"And the LORD God took the man, and put him into the garden of Eden to dress it and to keep it."
(Genesis 2:15)

STEWARDSHIP of the garden is where it all began. The garden is where we need to end up once again. It is that place of peace and tranquility the globe is searching for. All of man's wisdom is vain in comparison to God's ways. The plans of men are full of trial and tribulation. God's plans overflow with order and blessing.

He created us to be in fellowship and relationship with Him.

The New Testament book of Romans tells us that all men have the inborn propensity, desire, and ability to know God. *"For since the creation of the world His invisible attributes are clearly seen, being understood by the things that are made, even His eternal power and Godhead." (Romans 1:20 NKJV)* If that tendency, or need, is not filled by God, then a man will fill his soul with something else. "Something else" can be anything and everything offered in this world that keeps you away from God. All God wants from you is time to walk and talk with Him. He created us to be in fellowship and relationship with Him. He wants you to join Him in His garden.

When Adam and Eve were in the garden with God they all walked and talked together in the cool of the day. Adam had the amazing job of naming everything in God's creation *(Genesis 2:20)*. After that enormous job was completed, God created Eve as his companion. Eve was right beside Adam to assist him in every endeavor to keep and tend the garden. Can you imagine the immense task of naming and tending everything? I am not sure I can name everything in my house. I am certain I cannot tend to it all.

There is no doubt that in order to do such an enormous job Adam did not deal with of a lot of distraction or clutter in his brain which would have diminished his ability to concentrate. Nor did he have any conflicts to drain his energy. Adam and Eve lived in perfect balance and harmony with each other and their surroundings. They did not need to fix their conflict with the latest time saving devices or latest gadget. If they did, they would have realized that most of them just take away their ability to concentrate, not help it.

They were constantly focused on their relationship with each other and God.

There were no cell phones, PDA's, computers, traffic, angry co-workers, overdue bills, bad news (otherwise known as the evening news), or any other "convenience" of modern life. How could they get it all done? I am sure if they hired some help they could have done more. No. They accomplished everything and no doubt had a great time doing it as they were in one accord with each other and God himself.

They were constantly focused on their relationship, their needs, and their relationship with God. These things were what the garden was all about. If minor adjustments were needed, they made them without any anguish, harsh words, or debate. They tended their garden daily to keep it the way they wanted it and the way God wanted it.

It is not enough to just do the basic maintenance, our gardens need future planning. Good nurturing involves the steps of caring, maintaining, fixing, planning, achieving, and enjoying. When these steps are followed our garden prospers and does not fall into disrepair. Adam and Eve sowed and reaped a bountiful harvest during their time in the garden.

If not tended daily, weeds choke out life, peace, and fruitfulness.

Before the fall, weeds could never enter the garden due to ongoing, constant, and detailed care. Remember the thief that seeks to kill, steal, and destroy from *John 10:10*? He exists in every garden just waiting for his opportunity to bring destruction to your life. He cannot be allowed to succeed. If you neglect your garden the enemy will make advances against it. If you fail to sow goodness, mercy, kindness, and love you will not reap them. The enemy's weapons of anger, judgment, and disappointment will be harvested as a result of failure to care for your garden. Caretaking your life and the lives around you is a choice that must be made.

Your life and your family is your garden. As the cares of the world begin to pull your attention away from your garden you begin to lose focus toward your primary responsibilities of serving God, family, and your fellow man. If not tended daily, weeds begin to enter your garden and choke out the life, peace, and fruitfulness.

The parable of the sower talks of this concept from the physical world and relates it to the spiritual realm around us. Read it slowly, it is one of Jesus' most powerful teachings. Your seed must be planted in good ground to yield breakthroughs in your life.

The parable:

"On the same day Jesus went out of the house and sat by the sea. And great multitudes were gathered together to Him, so that He got into a boat and sat; and the whole multitude stood on the shore. Then He spoke many things to them in parables, saying: "Behold, a sower went out to sow. And as he sowed, some seed fell by the wayside; and the birds came and devoured them. Some fell on stony places, where they did not have much earth; and they immediately

sprang up because they had no depth of earth. But when the sun was up they were scorched, and because they had no root they withered away. And some fell among thorns, and the thorns sprang up and choked them. But others fell on good ground and yielded a crop: some a hundredfold, some sixty, some thirty. He who has ears to hear, let him hear!"

Matthew 13:1-9 (NKJV)

The parable explained:

"Therefore hear the parable of the sower: When anyone hears the word of the kingdom, and does not understand it, then the wicked one comes and snatches away what was sown in his heart. This is he who received seed by the wayside. But he who received the seed on stony places, this is he who hears the word and immediately receives it with joy; yet he has no root in himself, but endures only for a while. For when tribulation or persecution arises because of the word, immediately he stumbles. Now he who received seed among the thorns is he who hears the word, and the cares of this world and the deceitfulness of riches choke the word, and he becomes unfruitful. But he who received seed on the good ground is he who hears the word and understands it, who indeed bears fruit and produces: some a hundredfold, some sixty, some thirty."

Matthew 13:18-23 (NKJV)

Every area of our life requires stewarding.

God called Adam and Eve to care for His garden as its caretakers. God calls you to be the steward over your life. Stewardship is an important concept and is defined as the careful management of something under your responsibility like your marriage, family, or job. Every area of your life requires stewarding and balance is impossible without it. Your family must be cared for if your marriage is to succeed and your children to become successful. Your job and career must be managed wisely in order to prosper. Your home, vehicles, and property must be maintained to ensure all are in proper working order. If we do not steward our homes they will fall into disrepair. If we do not change the oil in our cars the engine will fail. In the same way, you must cultivate your relationship with God.

You must plant the Word of God you hear to ensure it takes root deep within your mind and spirit. *"Do not be deceived, God is not mocked; for whatever a man sows, that he will also reap." (Galatians 6:7 NKJV)* The law of sowing and reaping is in full effect every day of your life. You must tend to the Word of God as your personal garden.

Otherwise, if you do not tend it; the Word will be snatched away by the adversary. If you do not spend time with God you will not know what to do in times of crisis. Your prayers will be desperate cries for help instead of conversational assurance with your loving father. God will still answer desperate cries for help, but you will suffer for your lack of knowledge about who God is. Some people will even be destroyed by the works of Satan because their lives lack deeply planted truth. Without deeply planted truth, seeing a vision for a breakthrough life is a struggle.

My people are destroyed for lack of knowledge."
(Hosea 4:6 NKJV)

"Where there is no vision, the people perish."
(Proverbs 29:18)

We have all experienced conflict when areas of our life were not properly cared for. Relationships can be strained, finances can be stretched, and our peace of mind can be troubled. Likely, the conflict from lack of stewardship will make us feel out of control without a vision to regain it. Perhaps you are there right now. I know I have been there many times throughout my life. The choices you make will have an outcome. You must make good choices. If you sow anger you will reap anger. If you sow love you will reap love. If you sow bad stewardship, bad results will occur.

Ten dollars of stewardship

I once owned an old 1977 Jeep CJ5 that had an electrical malfunction. The malfunction would kill the motor and the jeep would come to a standstill. It would nearly always restart after a few minutes. Since I mainly used it for recreation I didn't fix it. I knew I should, but I didn't bother.

I was out driving one night on a busy stretch of road and the Jeep motor stopped in a very busy intersection. I had no power, no lights, and could not get out due to the narrow road and high walls surrounding me. I was nearly rear-ended by several speeding motorists. The entire time I was praying very loudly and kicking myself for not fixing a simple problem. By God's grace (and authoritative prayer) the engine started and I immediately zoomed out of the intersection and straight into my garage at home. My lack of stewardship almost got me killed.

My engine only needed a minor correction. In fact I went and bought the needed part the next morning. The part only cost ten dollars. I put my life in jeopardy as well as the lives of others on the road for a ten dollar part. How would my family have reacted if I had been in a serious auto accident or worse? I cannot imagine.

Looking back, it makes me feel quite foolish. It is our refusal to acknowledge and make minor adjustments that breeds conflict in our life. Pride is what keeps us from simple change. *Proverbs 16:18* tells us that pride will bring you low. Refusing to make small, daily adjustments to your attitude or life will be detrimental. Minor adjustments in your garden are not difficult. Dealing with large problems caused by ignoring them over a long period of time will be.

Take responsibility

We must take responsibility for our life if we are out of balance. Casting blame on our wife, children, or others for the things that do not work out only drives everything further out of balance and away from breakthrough. God expects us to be responsible as an adult expects a child to be responsible. The world is full of people who blame everyone else for their situations or problems. Casting blame is the easy way out. Taking the time to understand the problem, be accountable for it, and taking steps to alleviate it will direct us to a breakthrough.

Sometimes casting blame is done out of fear of rejection or fear of failure. *"If God is for us, who is against us?" (Romans 8:31 NASB)* It is okay to ask for help. I make mistakes all the time and end up having to apologize or ask for assistance. No man is an island able to withstand the storms of life alone. Everyone needs someone and we all need God.

Proper stewardship takes effort but it is a high calling. Paul said that his authority was entrusted to him by Christ. *"For if I do this willingly, I have a reward; but if against my will, I have been entrusted with a stewardship. What is my reward then? That when I preach the gospel, I may present the gospel of Christ without charge, that I may not abuse my authority in the gospel. (1 Corinthians 9:17-18 NKJV)* Paul was telling us that his love for Christ alone is reason enough to be good steward over what he was entrusted with.

If weeds have entered our garden, it will take some time to get them out. How much time is devoted to cleaning the garden depends on you. For example, your garden may require five hours of maintenance per week and mine only two because I started cleaning many years ago. You must find the balance and give attention to what needs to be weeded first. What areas need more attention? Do you have areas that require too much attention?

Your garden is your life.

Remember, God's original garden was a place of peace and tranquility because it was in perfect balance. We all have the ability to steward our garden because God says we do. We just need to acknowledge it and start cultivating our gift. The Apostle Peter said *"As each one has received a gift, minister it to one another, as good stewards of the manifold grace of God." (1 Peter 4:10 NKJV)* Our gifts of love, kindness, gentleness, and consideration are not just for ourselves but to be shared with family, friends, and others.

Breaking through life's challenges to walk and talk in the garden is a matter of striking your balance and going beyond it. Adam and Eve did not struggle to overcome situations in the garden; they just did what they were supposed to do because they wanted to do it. God took care of their overflow and abundance. It is a partnership between God and you. You do your part; He does His part. In fact, He even helps you do your part. You have the better deal.

Balance exists when your garden becomes well-maintained. Weeds do not infiltrate it and throw it out of balance. Breakthrough is achieved when the tending of the garden becomes part of who you are. You inwardly and outwardly know what you need to do and just accomplish it. Remember, your garden is your life. With a strengthened relationship with God it becomes second nature to make all of the minor adjustments to maintain it. You simply walk and talk to God in the cool of the day, person to person.

> *"Every good and perfect gift is from above, coming down from the Father of the heavenly lights, who does not change like shifting shadows."*
>
> *(James 1:17 NIV)*

STEWARDSHIP

"And the Lord God took the man, and put him into the Garden of Eden to dress it and to keep it."

(Genesis 2:15)

Chapter 16 Reflection

1. What does my personal garden look like?

   _____

   _____

   _____

2. Am I regularly tending my garden? Do I have some weeds to pull?

   _____

   _____

   _____

3. What steps do I need to take to bring my garden in line with God's?

   _____

   _____

   _____

4. How can I keep my garden alive with the Word of God?

   _____

   _____

Prayer to repeat out loud:

"Lord, thank You for teaching me to tend my garden with the mind of Christ. Thank You that I am a good steward over my time, talent, property, and relationships. Help me to represent Jesus in all my actions and opportunities to advance God's kingdom on the earth. In Jesus name, Amen."

CHAPTER 17

PEOPLE

"First cast out the beam out of your own eye; and then you will see clearly to cast out the speck out of thy brother's eye."

(Matthew 7:5)

PEOPLE are extremely important to each of us. We learn from people. We are related to people. We love people. We are examples for people to follow. We are led by people.

People are also the biggest area of struggle for most of us. Knowing them, loving them, working with them, sharing with them, and talking to them bring unique experiences for each of us. People are a big challenge because they are everywhere we are. The good news is that conflict with people is an arena where we have a significant amount of control. Understanding how we relate to others will keep God's purpose for our life in focus.

Our uniqueness makes us special.

The stress and strife experienced with others can cause you to ignore, reject, or neglect the call of God on your life. It is important to understand that all people have a call on their lives given by our Creator. You can see it everyday with those around you. Each individual has unique talent, personality, and intelligence.

God did not create victims only victors. God created us all in His special image *(Genesis 1:16)* and each one of us is equally important to His plan and purpose. In order to live my life fully, I need each and everyone I meet as much as they need me. God is all about relationships. He sent His only Son to die for you to enjoy a relationship with Him. Just as we need other people, we need God and His relationship. When you are in relationship with God, your other relationships will become more meaningful.

> *"For God so loved the world, that He gave his only begotten Son, that whosoever believeth in Him should not perish, but have everlasting life."*
>
> *(John 3:16)*

Because God loves diversity He gave some gifts to teach, to preach, to serve, to give, to support, to build, to invent, and many more abilities. Conflict comes in when our talents and time compete with the gifts of others and we don't know how to balance the two.

How you react is within your control.

There is truth in the statement, "You can choose your friends but not your family". You may not have control over who your relatives are but you do have a choice of who to marry, where to work, who to hang out with, what to hear, what to watch, and so on. When you add it up, you have influence over the majority of interpersonal relationships and outside influences experienced in life in, regard to you. Make no mistake, although you have influence, you do not have control over what other people do, say, or how they act. But how you react to them and what you choose to do about the situations that come up in life is within your control. Knowing this can make all the difference in life.

In the year 2000 I was offered the opportunity to live and work in New York City. At the time of the offer, we were living in a small Texas town called Bastrop which is outside of Austin. We were happily enjoying our church, friends, and growing family. I have to tell you,

Texas is a great place with some of the friendliest people you will ever meet. When the offer came for a transfer my wife and I just looked at each other, "That must be the devil. We don't want to move to New York City." I had been there on business trips and knew about all of the hustle, bustle, bad weather, and expense of living there.

Never say never when God is in the mix.

Why would we move? We had a happy and peaceful life in small town Texas. Surely God would never ask us to change it. So I rejected the offer and did not think much more about it. Does anyone out there know that God has a sense of humor? Never say never when God is in the mix.

About a year later during her prayer time, Gretchen felt a move was about to happen. She had not told me as she was continuing to seek God about it. I had the same prompting as well but also had not spoken to her. Ignoring something does not make it go away. A few weeks later the call came again about a transfer to New York City.

With the reality of the offer, we submitted it to prayer with some close friends as well as our pastor. Everyone came back with the same answer. Pack the bags folks, the Willard's are moving to New York City. What we did not know is how much we were going to miss home-made ranch dressing, fried dill pickles, and good salsa. But we would soon discover authentic Italian and Chinese food.

We were sent off by our church in Texas with the blessings and goals of being missionaries to the New York area. Our move was in February, 2003 which was a little over a year past the September 11 attacks. We felt strongly we could help people and looked forward to joining a local church in the New York area.

Things were looking up.

With a feeling of wonder and excitement, mixed with some fear and trepidation, we arrived and plugged in. God was with us throughout the transition and during our time there. We experienced immense favor with both God and man in our local church and in my job as a Chief Financial Officer for a division of a large consulting company in Midtown Manhattan. Things were looking up and it wasn't just the tall buildings. We ended up loving the area and the people.

After three great years, my company was purchased by a larger corporation and the upper management structure changed. All of the managers I worked with moved on to the parent company or left the organization. New managers came in and started making changes. I spent much of my time showing several new managers the ins and outs of the organization as well as introducing them to the many people I knew throughout the company. For a time everything seemed to be just fine and the blessings continued to flow.

At first my new manager was a cooperative team player with me and the rest of the staff. As time progressed his attitude became more distant and aloof toward me in particular. He began cutting me out of management meetings and suggesting staff changes that I felt were not in the company's best interests. I always voiced my opinions honestly and professionally even though I knew they were not agreed with. After several of these conversations the staff issues were dropped but I became more uncomfortable with the style of executive management we now had. I didn't agree with it but continued my support and focused on advancing the company but conflict increased.

Prior to the acquisition, my staff and I were always very informed about the happenings and data throughout the company. As more time progressed it became more difficult to get any information from the executive management team. People do not like re-creating something that should be easy to get. As a manager with dozens of employees, I was feeling intense pressure from both my staff and the people I reported to. My staff didn't like the new manager's rules that made their job more difficult and I was trying to work with him to facilitate a better relationship with everyone. I was having people conflict from many directions. Conflict between two groups of people is very difficult to navigate, especially when you are in the middle.

But at home and as a family our church activities were increasing. The company was paying for my Masters degree in business, the kids were growing, the birds were singing, the sun was shining…then wham! Conflict with people showed up on the scene in a big way.

I was flooded with emotions of fear, anger, and worry.

On an otherwise normal summer day at a scheduled management meeting with my supervisor, he bluntly stated that the company was going in a different direction and I was no longer needed. Essentially, thank you for your years of service and sacrifice; have a nice life. It was completely unexpected and I was flooded with emotion. Should I yell? Throw him out the window? (Our offices were on the eighth floor). Object? Laugh? Cry? And so on. I hate to admit it, but calling on the Lord at that moment was not in the forefront of my mind and the view from the window was looking mighty nice. Thankfully, the Holy Spirit and my professionalism prevailed and I left the office without a big incident.

On the way home I was flooded with emotions of fear, anger, and worry. I was distraught. What about the kids? What about the ministry? How can we pay the bills? Lord, have you abandoned us?

I took the next day in prayer with my wife and pastor, Scott Brown. I was in desperate need of support and encouragement. After some time of group prayer Pastor Scott Brown came over to me, took off my Timex and placed his Rolex on my wrist. He then spoke words into my life that I have never forgotten. "God wants you to know that you have done everything He has asked you to do. In the business world, after you have completed service to a business, you receive a gold watch. Here it is". He then placed his Rolex watch on my wrist.

Wow, what a blessing in a time of need. This was no ordinary gift. Pastor Scott's Rolex had been special to him. He waited many years to afford one. In my time of immense personal crisis he gave it to me as a gift. He was an instrument used by God to remind me that conflict with people and the circumstances it causes is only as temporary as we want it to be. God is always looking out for us. While I was feeling sorry for myself God blessed me in a very unique way to take my mind off of the natural and on His supernatural. *"For My thoughts are not your thoughts, nor are your ways My ways." (Isaiah 55:8 NKJV)* God never does things the way we would.

God is never caught by surprise.

That is how our God operates – supernaturally and abundantly. In times of trouble and distress He pours out His gifts and blessings to aid us. Did I really need a Rolex? In the natural, perhaps I did not. In the spirit, absolutely yes I did! To this day when I need encouragement or need to remember that God is for me I put that Rolex on and praise God for his goodness. Loosely translated, that means I wear it all the time because I need daily encouragement from God.

Don't lose sight of the message here. It is not about a Rolex. It is about how God meets us in our conflict with people and provides the way out. He gives exactly what we need exactly when we need it. In this sense, God is always on "time". (Hopefully I do not have to explain that.)

Never forget, God is always aware of your conflicts with others before you are and nothing catches Him by surprise. I still had many friends in executive positions within the organization and after some phone calls and conversations, the pink slip for me was reversed at a higher level. If you try to fight all your battles alone you will lose the majority of them.

Submit to the higher level of authority and always do the right thing with integrity. God defends the righteous. *"I have not seen the righteous forsaken, nor his descendants begging bread." (Psalms 37:25 NKJV)*

Our time in New York was over and within a few days I received a transfer out of my division and we moved to Fort Collins, Colorado. The people within the company that I had great relationships with took me right past balance and assisted me to a breakthrough with continued employment. It truly made me appreciate the golden rule and how important it is to treat others as you would like to be treated *(Matthew 7:12)*. In my personal crisis, many people came to my assistance.

We were sure God sent us.

When the excitement and work of the move wore off, I realized I was still very troubled with the doubts, fear, and anger the entire experience had left with me. I was in immense personal conflict from a major incident of people conflict. I found myself questioning everything. Weren't we called by God to be in New York City? What will happen to the ministry we were involved in? What about our children? Where will my career go from here? Can we ever recover? Why didn't I expect this? I should have planned better. I should have known!

We knew God sent us to the area to make a difference for His kingdom and to help others. However, instead of feeling victorious I was dealing with levels of unforgiveness and anger toward my former boss that I had really never experienced before. I was torn from the inside out and I truly could not get away from my anger because he completely changed my life in an instant.

During prayer over many months I repeatedly gave my feelings to the Lord. I didn't want all my anger toward my former boss. I released it over and over but soon found myself meditating on the injustice of the entire situation. My anger immediately returned.

After a few more months of this back and forth, I heard the Holy Spirit say this to me loudly in my spirit. *"Forgive them. They know not what they do. (Luke 23:24) I have loved them while they were unlovely. I chose to love them before they loved Me. Bless them that curse you, do good to them that hate you, and pray for them which despitefully use you, and persecute you."* (Matthew 5:44)

I knew immediately those words were directed right at my situation with my former boss. The Holy Spirit continued to minister to me and I heard this regarding him, *"I love him as I love you, as a son. Pray for his soul that he may believe in me and not perish"* These simple words define our basic job as Christians. We are to love the unlovely into the Kingdom of God.

Whoa! That stopped me cold. In the many months since we left New York while I was busy harboring anger and resentment; God needed me to pray for the salvation of my former boss. Due to my personal pain and rejection, I had lost sight of the entire reason God sent us to New York in the first place. We were missionaries sent to help people but I had excluded my former boss because he hurt me and my family. I loved others God brought into my life while we lived in the Northeast, just not him. My former boss deserved my best, not my worst.

Let's face it, God is into people.

God then brought to my remembrance various individuals we ministered to while we were there including salvations and the miracles we experienced; just to remind me further why we were moved to New York. Immediately I repented for my unforgiveness and lack of faith toward my former boss. (Repenting is simply turning away from what you were doing toward what God wants you to do.) I didn't realize that I was unhappy with myself. I felt like a failure for a long time. Having unforgiveness for any length of time is unhealthy and I carried it for many months. I started to pray for my former boss and saw the entire situation from God's perspective. My heart mended and over time I became free. I was free from the bondage of anger, unforgiveness, and rejection.

You need to like you.

There is one person in particular that causes you the most problems: *smile in the mirror and they will smile right back at you.* We each have a unique ability to make our personal situations more challenging than they need to be; especially where others are concerned or involved. All conflict you have with others originates with you.

The most important person in life to avoid conflict with is you.

Simply put, you need to like you. Many people go through life in personal conflict. They are not happy with how they look, how tall they are, how much they weigh, the decisions they have made, or how they feel. God made you and He thinks you are important. He loves you, me, and everyone else on the planet. Like overcoming self-induced conflict, we need to like ourselves before we can like others and others can like us.

I realized that it is not what happens to us or what people do to us; it is what we do about it. Overcoming conflict with people depends on us. How we respond to our adverse circumstances makes all the difference. Does our response glorify God or Satan? I want to freely glorify God and help His people.

"If the Son sets you free, ye shall be free indeed."

(John 8:36)

Let's face it, God is into people. We are all over the planet. We are here to stay and cannot be avoided. You cannot control anyone but that special person in the mirror: "me, myself, and I". You must be prepared when other people make decisions that impact or influence you.

PEOPLE

"First cast out the beam out of your own eye; and then you will see clearly to cast out the speck out of thy brother's eye."

(Matthew 7:5)

Chapter 17 Reflection:

1. Who am I in conflict with?

_____

_____

_____

2. What choices do I make that brings balance to my relationships?

_____

_____

_____

3. Do I judge others? If so, who? And why?

_____

_____

_____

Prayer to repeat out loud:

"Lord, thank You that the power of Your Holy Spirit gives me the strength and ability to love others instead of judging them. They are just like me, seeking answers for their life. Let me be a light and example of Your light and love for people. In Jesus name, Amen."

CHAPTER 18

THE JOB

"You will eat the fruit of your labor; blessings and prosperity will be yours."

(Psalm 128:2)

THE Job is where you spend a great majority of your waking life. Have you ever thought about how many hours you spend at work in a lifetime? Think about it, many of us go to work at least eight hours per day, five days a week for forty five years or more. That's roughly about 100,000 hours of work in a career. I sure hope you like your job.

Have you ever complained about your job? Do you dislike your job? Why? Have you ever analyzed the reasons for or against it? Is it the job or is it something inside of you? There is a drastic difference. Life is too short to dislike your job or some aspect of it.

Barter – Is it a good trade?

Before currency was the standard to exchange goods and services the barter system was in place. In fact, the barter system is alive and well today. Barters occur where one person "exchanges" their goods or services for another's goods or services. Value is determined based on what is being bartered and how much either item/service is needed by another.

What do you expect from your work?

What does your work expect from you?

People go to work for an expected amount of time and receive an amount of money. That is barter. Your time in exchange for a company's money is the transaction. Is the transaction worth it to you? It has to be for your needs to be met. You sacrifice a large amount of time to work during your lifetime.

How much you are paid is determined by what you have to offer in barter or trade. For example, a company may place a high value on a skilled electrician if installing lighting is their main business. A skilled electrician would likely receive a higher wage than an administrative helper. On the other hand, a financial services firm places much higher value on a skilled administrative helper than an electrician.

Think about all of the transactions you do on a daily basis. At their root, a barter exchange is occurring in every circumstance. You exchange food at a restaurant for the cash money in your wallet or purse. You pay for gasoline from the wages you earned by exchanging your time to your employer. You create, fix, design, or advise in return for money or other form of payment.

So what does an employer expect for their payment of time for your services? It is simple; if an employee is paid for eight hours of work then an employer expects eight hours of work. If the barter exchange of time for money is not kept by either party a breach of employment contract results. One party is essentially stealing from the other. It is an unbalanced barter exchange that causes many of the work conflicts experienced by people. One side of the barter is not providing their equal share of exchange.

1. *How do you view your work?*
2. *Do you care about the people you work with?*
3. *Do they care about you?*

How do you view your work? If you look forward to going to work every day you are probably have your perfect job. Perhaps you even view it as your place of ministry. Do you care about the people you work with? Are they like family or part of your personal success team? If so, then you are working in breakthrough employment. A bad case of the work doldrums may mean that it is time to shine the shoes and update the resume or take a class for more training. Why are you doing something you dislike? You give an immense amount of time, talent, and energy in exchange for a paycheck and some benefits. Is the company getting the better deal? Are you getting the better deal? Is it a fair trade off?

Work: It can be everything, yet nothing…

You may have heard the story of the person who spent all of his time at work. He never had time to be with friends and family. He rarely went to church and always missed or canceled personal appointments. Promises were often broken and apologies rare. Work was always on his mind no matter the event or location. Perhaps you may even know this person, or several of them. I know people like this.

Before realizing it, the children grew up and moved away. The marriage did too. With the marriage so went the finances. Not to worry, there was always work to fall back on. It was the old standby, tried and true. Work received all the personal commitment and its bond with the worker was stronger than anything else in life. Strangely, the work was never satisfied and always raised the bar to unachievable standards. There was always another deal, more money to make, more deadlines to satisfy.

On his death bed when the reality of a life wasted came crashing down, this person finally realized what he missed. His life was spent pursuing his job always wishing there was more time at the office – just one more report to the shareholders and I would have been anointed king of the world. (Sorry, that job is already taken). Do we have time for one more real estate deal? Is there time for two more yards of concrete, or five more feet of roofing? Can we get any more products out today? Imagine the bonus I will get if I stay just two more hours.

As it would be with all of us, the regrets and final thoughts are for the people, time, and places that never were and never will be. Love and relationships were never mended. Time lost is very difficult to recover.

Underpaid or under committed?

Working too much may not be your conflict. Perhaps you do not think you are paid enough. Maybe you are underpaid and underappreciated. It does happen, but can you honestly answer that you have been faithful in all of your job requirements? Or have you been slack arriving on time or taking too many personal breaks? Having these behaviors will cause conflict in your life and work life. Or perhaps it is a mathematical issue. You may spend more than you make, causing a financial conflict in your life not related to your job. But your job gets the blame. We will talk about financial conflict more in the next chapter.

Perhaps you feel inferior at your job or have hit a ceiling where promotion and advancement have ceased. You may have conflict over whether or not to go back to school for more qualifications or to seek another job. Maybe you just don't like someone you work with or have an unreasonable supervisor. Maybe you are afraid to make a change due to the economy and your financial responsibilities.

Sometimes out of our stress and perceived financial necessity we take a job that God never intended us to have. Other times, we can be in a job that is not good for us due to past history. For example, if you are repulsed by the smell of garbage, perhaps working at a landfill is not for you. Balance starts with determining whether or not you need change in your work life.

Work is an example set out by God himself.

To have balance in our work life we must find a job where we make a difference, not just exist to get a paycheck. Being employed helps give us significance and helps us feel important. Significance is the key for enjoying what we do and staying motivated to keep doing it. If you enjoy what you do for a living your outlook is more positive. Work does not drain your energy and you gain confidence from doing a good job.

Work is an example set out by God. He worked for the first six days of creation before there was rest (Genesis Chapter 1). Imagine if God did not enjoy His job for those first six days. What would our world be like? It would likely be incomplete and not function very well. (Be careful not to confuse the issues mankind creates every day with the beauty and perfection of God's creation...)

Your work life and career is vitally important. We spend time that takes us away from family and leisure. God wants us to work. He does not want us idle. Idleness leads to boredom and poverty. *"In all labor there is profit, but mere talk leads only to poverty." (Proverbs 14:23)* Idleness tarnishes our self confidence and confidence toward God.

Change: It's up to you.

In my early career I had a job with difficult hours and an angry boss. I did not enjoy going to work and didn't enjoy it while I was there. When I would get home I would rehash all of the challenges during the day to Gretchen. I could not see myself staying in this job if I wanted to enjoy the other parts of my life. Soon an opportunity presented itself and I took a job with another company. It was a few hours away in a different town and we had to move. Moving is not always easy but for my family and situation, the new job was a great decision. I had balanced my work life with my personal life and started a job I enjoyed going to everyday. Sitting and complaining was never going to change my situation. Sometimes action is needed. Moving or changing jobs can be a sacrifice, but for me it was a blessing that brought my family closer together.

Character Counts

It is also important do our job with character. Some people have work conflict because they have a bad attitude. No employer or co-worker

enjoys difficult employees or bosses. I know when I have managed
people in the past, the ones I least enjoyed were always complaining
and criticizing the work or co-workers. Because their attitude comes
from within, there is really nothing a company can do to assist their
happiness. Money will not fix them and neither will a new position.
They must decide to fix themselves. Happiness comes easily if you like
your job.

As the old saying goes, "Figure out what you love to do and then
find out how to get paid for it." Do you like what you do? If so, work
will not be a burden or chore. Your fellow employees will be added value
to your life and you will be an example to them.

"Figure out what you love and find out how to get paid for it!"

1. *What do you like to do?*
2. *Is there an industry that pays for what you do?*
3. *Is there an opportunity for you to create your own demand
   for your services or skills?*

Jesus bartered his life in exchange for the eternal salvation of our souls.

Jesus bartered His life in exchange for the eternal salvation of our
souls. Jesus balanced His immortality with walking for a short time as
a man on earth experiencing all manner of trial and temptation. He
balanced the weight of mankind's sin with the Father's absolute purity
and power. His goodness was exchanged for our salvation. His job was
to be the breakthrough for all of us.

No one could take advantage of Jesus without His permission.

Jesus' job was to be the Savior and redeemer for all mankind. He
knew it was His place and position. His path enabled Him to walk in

spiritual and physical authority wherever He went. No one was able to take advantage of Him or overcome Him without His willful permission. Can you imagine if Jesus was walking along with the disciples and decided that He did not want to show up for work the next day. Say what? We never imagine that Jesus could fail to show up for work. After all, He had responsibilities to live up to.

Yet day after day many of us shrink back from our daily responsibilities because we may not feel like it or believe it another's responsibility. God thought our soul was important enough to send His only Son to die for us. He followed through to the end. Even when the situation became difficult Jesus kept going. Job breakthrough waits in patience, perseverance, and consistency. Have you ever noticed that the biggest complainers in life never earn the promotion or receive advancement? Their employer is not able to trust them with any more responsibility. Grumbling, mumbling, and complaining are the short path to nowhere in particular.

After all, if a person is not happy with what he has, why would anyone expect him to be happy with more? Managers and business owners are not likely to advance or promote anyone that is always looking for something better. *"Don't love money; be satisfied with what you have. For God has said, "I will never fail you. I will never abandon you." (Hebrews 13:5 NLT)*

If you are grateful with what you have but feel there is more you can do; you may need to improve yourself in order to take another step forward. All the people in jobs you think are wonderful did not get there right out of high school or college. They worked to gain experience, studied to improve their skills, became educated, certified, licensed, and proved they could do the job.

The Kingdom of God works like that. Advancement comes to those that show diligence, obedience, and honesty in their tasks. God rewards those who seek Him. *"He is a rewarder of them that diligently seek Him."* *(Hebrews 11:6)*

Contentment

Discontented people stay stuck. Even if you know you are at the wrong job, if you are faithful and content with it, God will promote you beyond it. Impatience and contentment cannot co-exist. After you are content where you are God will meet you. *"I have learned to be content whatever the circumstances." (Philippians 4:11 TNIV)*

In order to have success in life you must be content with your work situation. Contentment opens the door to blessing. Life is too short to plod through in misery. There are plenty of jobs that will bring you satisfaction and contentment. Customize your wants and needs with employment. A job that fits your lifestyle, schedule, and family is worth its weight in gold.

If something is holding you back from change, such as debt; consider downsizing where you can. A job should never be just a responsibility to make ends meet or pay bills. A fulfilling job will be a blessing to you, not an obligation.

> *"But godliness with contentment is great gain."*
>
> *(1 Timothy 6:6)*

The Bible even promises personal rewards if we act with integrity.

> *"The righteous man walks in his integrity; His children are blessed after him.*
>
> *(Proverbs 20:7 NKJV)*

> *"And whatsoever ye do, do it heartily, as to the Lord, and not unto men"*
>
> *(Colossians 3:23)*

I estimate that 75% of you are in the right job and 25% of you are in the wrong job. Of the 75%, if you feel unhappy it is likely from a lack of contentment. If you adjust your perspective on how your job is a blessing to your life, your attitude will improve. The other 25% of you need to plan carefully. Do not do anything without consulting the Lord. Consider why you are in your current job and plan the breakthrough to your next opportunity as a partner with God.

Breakthrough an ordinary work life by bringing an extraordinary attitude everywhere you go. True promotion is from the Lord. It comes through hard work, integrity, and submission to authority.

If you want to succeed, succeed at being the person God is asking you to be!

THE JOB

"You will eat the fruit of your labor; blessings and prosperity will be yours."

(Psalm 128:2)

Chapter 18 Reflection:

1. Am I respecting my work boundaries by getting to work, class, or my responsibilities on time? Why or why not?

   _____

   _____

   _____

2. Am I giving my best to my employer in return for my salary/ wages? Why or why not?

   _____

   _____

3. What can I do to make my job more enjoyable?

4. Do I consider my job my ministry?

Prayer to repeat out loud:

"Father, thank You that You have provided a job to meet and fulfill my needs, the needs of my family, and the needs of others. I purpose to excel at my job and work as unto You, not men. True promotion comes from the Lord and I am grateful that I work for You. In Jesus name, Amen."

Six Practical Ways to Achieve Work Success:

1. **Get to work on time:** Getting to work on time will ease great stress on you. Timely arrival will allow you to proactively plan your day and execute your tasks. Starting out behind is never good for overcoming adversity. (Your managers generally do not like it either.) When you get to work on time you are much more likely to leave on time. Getting to work late causes many

people to work more hours to make up the time as well as ensure a good impression with management.

2. **Take the first 10 minutes:** Start each work day to preview what is before you. Do you have any deadlines? Which task has priority over another? Are there any important emails or voice mails that need attending to? Do you have all of your tools or supplies? Of course, the realities and complexities of your job never quite allow you to stick to the plan. If that is the norm, then do not be surprised when it happens. Expecting disruptions and deviations can give you great peace within the framework of your job.

3. **Do not argue:** If you disagree, do it with courtesy and with professionalism no matter what work you do. As with all inter-personal relationships, it takes two to have an argument. One sided arguments do not last very long. We should approach our work situation in accordance with the following scripture:

> *"Whatever you do, work at it with all your heart, as working for the Lord, not for men, since you know that you will receive an inheritance from the Lord as a reward. It is the Lord Christ you are serving."*
> *(Colossians 3:23-24 NIV)*

Working for the glory of God brings you peace and authority over every situation that comes. When adversity does happen, choose to be proactive and positive about your role in solving it. Managers like problem solvers, not problem makers or announcers. Take responsibility for any errors you committed and be realistic about what can actually be accomplished within a given time frame. The right attitude can take you far in a career.

4. **Communicate:** Even if you cannot accomplish a task within a deadline, it will generally turn out fine if you take the time and effort to communicate with all parties about progress, or lack

thereof. People, especially managers, do not like to be surprised, so keep them informed. Christ taught in parables but no one wants you to. Don't let your job be a mystery to supervisors.

5. **Make a difference:** Show why you are a good employee. Look for ways to make your company, employer, or workplace more efficient. Efficiency saves money and creates opportunity. Additionally, keep your job skills current. If periodic training is required, do it early. If there is a need for special certification or schooling in your job, volunteer to get it. Initiative tied together with qualifications is the main reason for advancement and promotion.

6. **Take your final 10 minutes:** Before leaving at the end of each day to organize your desk, vehicle, work area, and leave it clean. Doing so makes your following day more pleasant. You will not walk into a messy area that screams you are already behind schedule. Start your day prepared and end your day prepared. Preparation will identify critical tasks that will need addressed the next day so they are not overlooked.

Chapter 19

Money & Debt

"Owe no man any thing, but to love one another."
(Romans 13:8)

MONEY is not the root of evil, just a lack of it is. Actually, that is not true nor is it an accurate quote. However, money and money related issues are a top reason for marital conflict, life conflict, people conflict, and all other conflict. As the old saying goes, "Money won't make you happy, but it will give you the ability to find something that does." We can chuckle at this, but we must be very careful how we approach money.

Why all the focus on money? Without it, not much can be done in life either for the gospel, yourself, or others. The world economy is based on it. Many are preoccupied with it. Wall Street is obsessed with it. The government needs it and taxes its citizens to get it. People break the law for it. Some go through years of school to get more of it. Laborers give their sweat and backs for it. The executive works long hours to attain more of it. Some people hoard it. Some people over-spend it. Workers build in exchange for it. If I gave you $100 dollars right now you likely would not refuse it.

The devil would like us to have no money and be in total financial conflict. No one is put on this earth to conquer it all, horde all the wealth, or hurt others for personal gain. Some people actually do these things but it comes with a terrible price; their soul.

"What does it profit a man if he gains the whole world and loses his soul?"

(Mark 8:36)

Mark 8:36 asks a very good question and it has a very simple answer. The answer is nothing. It profits nothing. Nada, zero, zilch. Oh yes, there may be fame and fortune for a time, but the view from the top of a mountain of wealth or power that is gained dishonestly is bleak. Prosperity and success are not just measured in monetary terms but also in spiritual terms. The following scriptures emphasize God's idea on this concept. God's prosperity is partnered with integrity, character, and honesty.

"Unless the Lord builds the house all labor in vain."

(Psalm 127:1)

"The hand of the diligent shall rule."

(Proverbs 12:24)

If we build something through honesty, dedication, and focused application, it can profit for all of eternity. Dishonest gain may bring wealth for a season, but it is sure to crumble because it has no foundation. *Dishonest money dwindles away, but he who gathers money little by little makes it grow." (Proverbs 13:11 NIV)*

Most people work and only want enough to balance the checkbook, pay the bills, and buy a few nice things. But God wants us in financial breakthrough with more money than we need so that we are able to meet the concerns of others.

God wants you to prosper. The Lord never wants his children to go without provision. In the *Exodus,* the children of Israel left Egypt loaded down with silver and gold. In the desert, He provided sustenance by raining down manna from the sky and giving water from rocks. The Bible tells us Solomon was the wealthiest man who ever lived. In the New Testament, church offerings are taken for the apostles to fund the further preaching of the gospel. The Bible states the Lord owns the cattle on a thousand hills and everything of value in the earth belongs to Him. *(Psalm 50:10)* With the wrong money perspective the Lord's hills will seem far away.

Debt is an unfortunate reality of modern life and is another form of conflict. There are different types of debt that need to be clarified. It is generally understood in society that certain types of debt are ok such as car payments and house payments. These are needed for living and getting to work. You can even deduct mortgage interest from your taxes. Bankers will tell you if the debt from your car and house is less than what you can sell it for then you are really not in debt. What if you cannot afford either payment? That seems like debt to me. The higher thought is to have the ability to pay it all off if necessary. God's standard is that you do not owe anyone any money.

Most people take on more debt than they can afford. The more debt that you have the higher your payments and cash expenditures will be. More debt increases the likelihood that any shortfalls will be covered by other types of loans such as credit cards. The more debt you acquire the greater your chance to become overwhelmed by it.

Mishandling money brings many sorrows and leads to debt. Loving money creates a desire to always have more. You cannot ever be content if money is your goal. Desiring money will lead you down the long road of debt.

> *"For the love of money is the root of all kinds of evil. And some people, craving money, have wandered from the true faith and pierced themselves with many sorrows."*
>
> *(1 Timothy 6:10)*

Debt means less freedom.

Banks were free with credit terms and for many years there were few who did not qualify for a loan. The "why wait for tomorrow when you can have it today" mentality fuels debt.

I can tell you the result of too much debt is that you will be you working more hours to pay it back. "I owe, I owe, and it is off to work I go." The downside to debt is high bills, collection calls, bankruptcy, marital problems, anger, frustration, anxiety, and no money. People have begun to realize debt has limitations but there is still plenty of it to go around.

God understood that debt is detrimental to our life. The apostle Paul clearly states this in *Romans 13:8* with the scripture, *"Owe no man any thing, but to love one another: for he that loveth another hath fulfilled the law."* Is your life in agreement with this scripture? For many years mine was not and it takes continual effort to walk it out even today.

I remember when we were first married as seniors at the University of Arizona. Until then we were each partially supported by parents. My parents felt we were too young to get married and if I was old enough to take a wife, then I could provide for one. The problem was that I was still in college and only had a part time job. After all, who needs money when you marry for love, right? Gretchen also worked part time also but there was not enough to make ends meet.

The late 1980's and early 1990's was the time that credit card companies started to target young adults in college. I still remember the signs and promotion booths on campus that were manned by successful looking students: "Sign up here to get a free T-shirt and new Visa card." Or, "Join today and receive a new backpack". Everyone needs a free T-shirt, so I took the plunge to plastic.

Due to our lack of cash and our desire to actually have a few possessions as a newly married couple; we started making up the difference with plastic. Credit cards carried us get between paychecks and helped us before we had full time jobs. Our credit cards even helped pay for our college tuition. We didn't go crazy and buy everything we wanted. But in spite of this, credit card debt overcame us one charge at a time. That's how it happens.

Unfortunately, what we didn't understand back then was that if we could not afford at the moment; what made us think we could afford to pay it off later? Let me tell you, it wasn't so obvious back then. Soon we managed to accumulate $10,000 on two cards. That is a large amount, and in the early 1990s it was crushing to our single income household.

I had to get out of debt.

A year later, I was working my first full-time job as a cost control accountant for a large mining company. Our $10,000 ball and chain was following us around. I ignored it because it made me feel depressed. I always managed to make more than the minimum payments but could never seem to get the balance down because we still used the cards. I soon began to realize I had a serious debt problem that was going to take years to pay off. I knew that the balance was going to hold us back from qualifying for lower interest rates, for car loans, and it might hinder our ability to buy our first home.

I had to get out of debt. In fact, I started to hate the debt itself, which is an important step toward financial balance. That certainly is the right motivation for a successful debt reduction plan. I began to explore my options. Being new to the workforce I had not managed to save any money. What could I do?

We reached out for help from a few family members that we thought might be sympathetic and understanding but no one was interested. I can understand their point of view not wanting to just bail us out for fear we would just get back into more debt. After some more late night discussions, I went to a great uncle of mine. My Uncle Pete had been a career Army Sergeant with nearly 40 years in the service. He lived very frugally and was a polite and organized man. Additionally, he had something I did not. He had discipline in his life and wisely managed his possessions. I was concerned that he would judge me harshly for getting into such a large amount of debt. He was, after all, an Army Sergeant. However, I knew I could not continue to manage our card balances so I decided to ask him for help.

I felt unworthy to actually receive help.

I slowly and painfully explained how we got into the situation. I held nothing back. He said to me, "How much do you need and what is your proposed re-payment plan?"

I had not really planned that far ahead because I felt unworthy to actually receive help and really never thought we would get it. Pride is the reason we do not want help or refuse to accept assistance. My uncle stated, "Everyone makes mistakes." Then he bluntly asked me if I was going to get back into debt. I exclaimed, "No way, never! I hate the feeling and how it weighs us down." He then proceeded to write me a check to pay off the balances and put me on a payment plan back to him. What a blessing.

> "But my God shall supply all your need according to his riches in glory by Christ Jesus." (Philippians 4:19)

I always paid more than he asked and never missed a payment. After a few years he called me and forgave the remaining balance because he felt we had proven our ability to make better decisions. We were very blessed by his help and I have managed to keep my promise to him to this day by not getting back into the debt pit.

It was "us" that got "us" into debt. It was going to take "us" changing our actions to get out.

We were very fortunate to have some assistance for getting out of our financial situation. However, it was "us" that got "us" into debt and it took "us" changing our habits and actions to get "us" out and stay out. While I am a supporter of credit cards for convenience, travel, and emergency money, I dislike the financial issues they create for many families that are not prepared for their potential pitfalls.

How do you view money?

Creating financial balance in your life starts with how you view money. As stated earlier, Jesus taught that money is not the root of all evil but the "love" of money is the root of all evil *"For the love of money is the root of all evil" (1 Timothy 6:10)* If one lusts and pursues after the goal of gain, usually laws are broken and innocent lives are also are damaged along the way. It is important to understand that God wants us to have enough to feed, clothe, and shelter our family; but He also wants us to have extra so we can meet the needs of others.

We are not to have extra at the expense of others. The "extra" is only entrusted to those that have been faithful with what they already have. *"And he said unto him, Well, thou good servant: because thou hast been faithful in a very little, have thou authority over ten cities." (Luke 19:17)*

Live within your means.

Living within your means is one of the most simple and effective ways to avoid money trouble in life. There is always a bigger house, a nicer car, and faster boat, newer golf clubs, or flashier jewelry. Leave the rat-race to the rats and spend your time on things that make a positive difference in your life and the lives of others. What are things that make a difference?

If you are in large amounts of debt be honest and think about how it grew to where it is today. Do you like to shop? Do you always need the best or newest thing? Are you trying to impress people? Get to the heart of why your debt exists. Solving any underlying issues of spending gives you the opportunity to bring your finances into balance for good.

Debt is a predator that eats away the joys of life and opens the door to misery. God does not want his children in debt or beholden to others. Debt restricts your ability to live a victorious life and limits your ability to help those beyond you.

Please understand that if you have debt by no means is this chapter meant to condemn or accuse. Many people have issues with debt as

I had my share. Most debt piles up from a multitude of small, easy, and simple transactions. Can you even remember all the purchases that add up to your monthly balances; even if you pay it off? Were they life enhancing bringing greater enjoyment than the angst that debt causes? I can think of very few situations where that can apply beyond an emergency life-saving situation.

Debt makes others rich.

Every time you pay interest on a loan or balance, someone else is making a profit off of the interest that you are paying. *"The rich ruleth over the poor, and the borrower is servant to the lender." (Proverbs 22:7)* Your payment plus interest equals wealth for another. Debt causes you to be an indentured servant to the debt holder. Essentially, you work for the people you owe.

So how do we balance our finances? Finances flow through every area of our life. To be out of balance is to be in trouble. Balance is the imperative first step for walking in abundance and any type of overflow. You will never get out of the red ink unless you understand what you have, how much you have, and where you want it to go. It is time to eliminate debt. Tithing is the first step to achieving financial balance.

The Tithe

We must tithe. As believers in Christ we are called to tithe. A tithe means one-tenth of our income is sown back into your local church. Lasting financial prosperity will never come to someone that does not tithe. A tithe shows our faithfulness to the Lord that we trust Him to take care of our need. In turn, it shows God can trust us with money. It shows your ownership and truly helps you belong to "your church" not the church. The tithe is part of God's master plan for our life and it teaches us discipline.

Pastors and church leaders need a salary. *A workman is worthy of his hire. (Matthew 10:10)* The utilities and equipment at church need to be funded. Missionaries need to be supported. We must all do our part. Otherwise you are essentially stealing from God. *"Will a man rob God? Yet you rob me. But you ask, 'How do we rob You?' In tithes and offerings."* (Malachi 3:8 NIV)

The church is only vibrant and alive due to the cooperative action of all its members. It is important to do your part. If you are a church participant you have ownership and responsibility in the success and vision at your church. *"For where your treasure is, there will your heart be also."* (Matthew 6:21)

I decided to tithe on faith alone.

I doubted the impact of the tithe when I was a new Christian. I thought that it seemed a bit excessive to give 10% of my income to the local church. After all, I was barely making it myself. However, God had already moved mightily in my marriage and family as a new believer so I decided to tithe on faith alone. Over the next year of our life we saw great financial increase in our life. I was promoted. A relative gave us a new car. We became more disciplined in our finances so we were able to help others in a way that we had never done before. Tithing was the first step to balance in our life and gave us a vision for stewardship over the income we had. The second step was making decisions to remove debt.

Debt or no debt? Which do you prefer?

Debt removal takes sacrifice and planning. If you are in debt, your debt did not accumulate overnight and it will take some time to get rid of it. You may need to change your lifestyle and habits. You will need to live within your ability or below to get rid of debt. It is one of the most important decisions you will make in your life.

As I stated before, I began to hate debt. I couldn't do anything I wanted to in life after piling up debt. I started to make choices to remove it forever. During what we call our "debt removal" phase (it came after our "debt accumulation" phase) I took inventory of what we needed and what was extra. I quickly noticed we owned two brand new cars with payments. It didn't take much more thinking to realize we didn't need them both. We sold one and bought an older, less expensive car with no payment. We used the extra income to pay off a few bills and put money into savings. We made more choices like this and soon significantly reduced our debt.

A good friend of ours sold most of what they had to get out of debt. They had accumulated so many "things" they became enslaved to monthly payments. To get out they sold a boat, a car, motorcycles, and even their house to achieve financial balance. They quit eating out and started shopping at discount stores. Their piece of mind became more important than all of the things they acquired.

Formulate a budget plan and follow it.

If you need help, there are many affordable professionals out there that can make sense out of it all. In my professional life, I have counseled and planned many budgets for those wanting to be free from the crushing feeling debt brings. Debt is not a respecter of persons. It doesn't care how much or how little money you have. Every person can and should have a budget that fits them. Do not buy something you cannot afford. If you don't have cash for it, say no to debt and the conflict it brings.

Even through it is still debt, houses and cars can be an exception to this rule. Why am I saying this when I stated earlier that these are still considered debt? There is a cost for living. Even if you don't own a house you still need to pay rent. If you don't own a car you still need transportation. There are basic living expenses that cannot be avoided.

However, don't overbuy (meaning – do not buy something that is too big or too expensive for your income) a house or a car. What can you really afford? What is practical for your life? Is it worth working your life away to pay for a house that is too big or a fancy car that just wears out?

Get ready, take a deep breath, you can do it. Make a budget. A budget is a simple plan that balances your income coming in with your expenses that you pay out. Take control of your financial health by understanding how much cash you have coming in every month and how much you have going out. A simple budget works like this:

A Simple Budget:

1. Make a list of your sources of income and add it up.
2. Make a list of your expenses (cash outflows) and add it up.

   a. Be honest. Check the actual numbers. Otherwise you will not put enough in to be realistic.

3. If your income is greater than expenses you are in good shape.
4. If your expenses are larger than your income:

   a. Review your list to see what can be removed.
   b. Make a plan to eliminate extra expenses.
   c. Figure out how to make more income.

The area where most people fail is they don't actually follow their budget. In order to create lasting change you must be committed. How much do you want it? How much do you want to eliminate your debt? Only you can do it. Get serious about taking control of your finances. It will take effort, time, and prayer. Keep it up and you will begin to see your breakthrough.

Breaking through into God's financial arena

The breakthrough comes when you participate in God's financial plan. Breakthrough occurs when you go beyond the discipline of just following a budget and having enough finances for yourself. The budget teaches discipline but the goal is to have so much we can give it away to others. Breakthrough exists in going beyond your needs and having more than enough for others.

Have you ever dreamed of having an overflow of finances that you could by a house or car for someone in need? How about helping a needy family buy clothes or put food on the table? Maybe the building project needs a silent benefactor – it could be you someday. God likes to meet the needs of others through His people. He wants to meet needs through you. Are you faithful? Can he trust you with money? He wants to.

> *"Give, and it will be given to you: good measure, pressed down, shaken together, and running over will be put into your bosom. For with the same measure that you use, it will be measured back to you."*
>
> *(Luke 6:38 NKJV)*

God is the God of more than enough but He needs our cooperation to do it. You and I are His hands and feet in the world. Breakthrough finances fund the Gospel of good news throughout the earth. They fund Bibles and missionaries for people that need them.

Breakthrough finances are having more than enough.

Believe God at His word. If you do, increase and breakthrough in your financial situation is His guarantee. Give your finances over to the Lord. Financial freedom is one of the most joyous feelings that exist in today's pressure filled world. Do not be the indentured servant to the world's system. *"Owe no man anything but to love him."* (Romans 13:8)

> *"Beloved, I wish above all things that thou mayest prosper and be in health, even as thy soul prospereth."*
>
> *(3 John 1:2)*

Money & Debt

"Owe no man any thing, but to love one another."

(Romans 13:8)

Chapter 19 Reflection:

1. Am I a good steward over the money God has given me? Why or why not?

_____

_____

_____

2. Do I consider my purchases over the long term? Why or why not?

_____

_____

_____

3. Do I have debt beyond my ability to pay it back? How can I reduce or remove it from my life?

_____

_____

_____

4. Do I include God in my finances? Do I tithe? Do I pray over my finances? Why or why not?

_____

_____

_____

Prayer to repeat out loud:

"Thank You Father that You are not only the Lord of my life but You are the Lord of my finances. I give the authority over my financial decisions to You and purpose to pray that my financial decisions are in agreement with Your Word. Bless my finances abundantly so all of my needs are met and I can give into the Kingdom to help others. In Jesus name, Amen."

CHAPTER 20

VICTORY

"But thanks be to God, which giveth us the victory through our Lord Jesus Christ."

(1 Corinthians 15:57)

VICTORY is our ultimate goal. It lines up exactly with God's definitive vision of restoring right relationship with us through Jesus. We were bought with the precious blood of Jesus and been given a precious gift called life. Our world was never meant to be a place of hardship, toil, and snares. There is no conflict within victory, but overcoming our conflict brings victory.

Webster's 1812 dictionary defines **victory** as follows:

Noun:

"The advantage or superiority gained over spiritual enemies, over passions and appetites, or over temptations, or in any struggle or competition."

Ironically, we would not know what victory feels like if we did not have some form of hardship, challenge, or difficulty. The agony of defeat should be only a temporary feeling, emotion, or circumstance. In fact, that agony occurs for only a mere moment in time and is the start to gaining victory. Hardships, challenges, and difficulties give us a powerful frame of reference from which to reach out to victorious living. Everything looks up when you have had a view from the bottom. God's amazing grace picks us up, dusts us off, and sets our feet upon solid ground to continue life's journey. Of course, the better plan God has for our life is to work with Him for the advancement of His kingdom so we do not have to hit the bottom.

Once you are at the top of your circumstances, it is much easier to stay there.

Have you ever stood in a valley and looked around to the surrounding hills or mountains? A valley is only a temporary stopping place on your way to the next summit in life. When you do reach the peaks, look back and really appreciate how far you have come. You realize the valley really was not as deep as it looked when you were in it. Once you are at the top of your circumstances, it is much easier to stay there. Walking in victory fills in the valleys and you live from one victory to another.

We have identified many areas of conflict, how they are caused, and how to avoid and remove them. We discussed that our conflicts are a result of choices we have made and how to balance our choices. Prioritizing our choices creates a more harmonious life and frees up our time which can be better spent serving our family, our friends, and our God.

Once our life becomes more balanced, we can take the next step and break through the drudgery and really start to live and enjoy life. Breaking through is not a one-time occurrence. It is a repetitive process of submitting our will to the plan of God. We must always focus on balancing away from conflict and its wasted-time. Breakthrough is focusing on God's victorious plan for our life. How do we do it? How do we keep our breakthrough?

Concentrate on what really matters to you in life.

The answer is simple. Concentrate on what really matters to you in life and stay away from everything else. If time with family is what you desire, pattern your hobbies and behavior toward your family. If alone time with God is most important to you, cut out all the non-essentials. God doesn't care about your busy work. It does not impress Him. In fact, God through His son Jesus set us free from all the bondage and cares of the world.

"If the Son sets you free, ye shall be free indeed."

(John 8:36)

Throughout our lives there are opportunities to fail or fall down. I believe that we have many more opportunities to succeed, overcome, prosper, enjoy, and live in victory! ***This book is dedicated those who desire a new outlook on life, have the courage to achieve it, and embrace the abundant life that God has for you.*** Man does not have all the answers, however, I have a relationship with the Man who does, and so do you.

God's spiritual laws are always at work and bring victory!

God has all of our answers and is just waiting on us to claim them. They are free and they are abundant. In Christ, we have the victory to all life. Thankfully, God's ways are not our ways. The designs and methods He has set up do not always make sense to our natural mind as they are spiritual and supernatural. However, our natural mind can be trained to be sensitive to God's spiritual laws the more time we spend reading the Bible and seeking His counsel. God's spiritual laws are always at work and they always work. His laws are straight-forward and never change but they come with a personal requirement. That requirement is a partnership. Partnerships require the cooperation of more than one person. God is one partner and you are the other.

God's blessings are ours for the taking to live a victorious life.

Scripture tells us that God's blessings are ours for the taking. He has set them before us to choose and live a victorious life. However, there is a corresponding action on our part to make them flow. God loves us with an everlasting love, but like any good parent, He will not do everything for us. Accomplishment through study, effort, action, work, and submission enables people to grow and excel.

Proverbs tells us that money easily gained is easily lost. The same is true of other blessings in life. If "things" or "items" are easily gained, stewardship over them is not generally as excellent as stewardship over items gained by challenge and hard work. If we work to earn something we generally take better care of it. I have learned through the years that good things come after good planning and hard work.

God does and can just bless people by His grace, but He prefers to work with us. If we learn to work with God, all of His wonderful blessings are poured out for us. There is a wonderful principle in this. As we learn to walk in the will of God for our own life, we start to notice the world around us and meet the needs of others. That is breakthrough living.

The truly overcoming life is not about money or things. The blessed life is about walking in the prosperity of God. God's prosperity exists in every part of our being: spirit, soul, body. It overruns our homes, jobs, family, finances, possessions, and most importantly people.

Life's choices lay before us. Choose life. *"I have set before you life and death, blessing and cursing;* **therefore choose life**, *that both you and your descendants may live."* (Deuteronomy 30:19 – my emphasis added) "You and your descendents" – make sure you get that phrase. Our decisions affect us today, our children tomorrow, and their children to come. Those same decisions impact the world today, tomorrow, and in the future.

Choose the Prince of Peace. Choose the small, daily tasks that truly make a difference. Pray for those around you. Give to those in need.

Let God invade your life. If we change nothing in our life, conflict will continue and there will always be a struggle for balance. Live boldly and step out to join God in His breakthrough. Live a life of victory. That is God's choice. The next choice is up to you.

- *Conflicts are situations that take us away from what we need to do.*
- *Balance is the ability to only take on and achieve what we are called to do.*
- *Breakthrough is the victorious life where we accomplish all God desires us to do.*

VICTORY

"But thanks be to God, which giveth us the victory through our Lord Jesus Christ."

(1 Corinthians 15:57)

Chapter 20 Reflection:

1. Am I living a victorious life? Why or why not?

_____

_____

_____

2. Why is it important that I am victorious?

_____

_____

_____

3. What steps can I take to bring more victory in my life?

_____

_____

_____

4. Am I willing to make the necessary changes in my life to bring about breakthrough?_____ What are those changes?

_____

_____

_____

Prayer to repeat out loud:

"Our Father in heaven, Hallowed be Your name. Your Kingdom come. Your will be done on earth as it is in heaven. Give us this day our daily bread. And forgive us our debts, as we forgive our debtors. And do not lead us into temptation, but deliver us from the evil one. For Yours is the kingdom and the power and the glory forever. Amen"

(Matthew 6:9-15)

ABOUT THE AUTHORS

DAVID WILLARD

DAVID Willard, MBA resides in Tucson, Arizona with Gretchen, his wife, and four children. During the Willard family travels around the United States, David has served as a deacon, marriage and family counselor, small men's group leader, children's leader, Sunday school teacher, Christian drama actor, and served on various church committees. He was previously a Chief Financial Officer in New York City and now is the president of his own consulting firm teaching business techniques and leadership to individuals and small companies.

David was born and raised in Arizona and loves the state and the climate. He met his wife while attending the University of Arizona. His activities and interests vary greatly from volunteering at his local church, teaching about Jesus, writing, coaching his kids, camping, speaking to local professional groups, and consulting with businesses and individuals. It is important to him that others succeed and get the most out of their life. David believes God has blessed us all richly and that He enjoys seeing His children do well with their relationships, careers, and family. There is a special place in his heart for Texas where three of his children were born and the seed of Christianity was rooted, cultivated, and nurtured by the wonderful people in his first church in Bastrop, Texas.

GRETCHEN WILLARD

Gretchen enjoys home schooling the four Willard children: Georgia, Savannah, Oran, and Truman. Home schooling is the most rewarding and challenging endeavor of her life.

Gretchen has served as a young wife and new mother's mentor, children's leader, marriage and family counselor, small group Bible instructor, Christian drama actress, and teacher.

She and David met at the University or Arizona where she graduated with a degree in finance. She has always enjoyed David's business interests and serves as his confident, advisor, and partner. She serves as the vice-president of the family consulting business and enjoys opportunities to help people get ahead in life.

Gretchen and David are jeep enthusiasts and enjoy anything to do with dirt roads, hiking, camping, or outdoor adventures. As an avid animal lover, Gretchen volunteers her time to help rescue animals in order to adopt them into permanent homes.

Her goal is to share the life changing love of Jesus with everyone she meets to help people get free from habits, attitudes, behaviors, and hurts from past experiences. She knows a future with Jesus is full of hope, peace, contentment, and joy if we learn to live each day walking in the love of God.